C#

Animation
&
FFmpeg

Jayasankar S

Contents

About the Author

 Jayasankar S is an IT professional with more than 15 years experiance in .NET technologies. He started as a software developer specializing in .NET and has since worked in various roles, such as Senior Software Engineer and Principal Engineer in different companies. He has worked on various projects throughout his career, including Image processing, PDF, Web, Database, and Mobile App development. Jayasankar holds an undergraduate degree in Physics from Kerala University and a Master's in Computer Applications (B' Level course) from NIELIT.

Preface

Welcome to my book C# Animation and FFmpeg. In this book, I aim to provide a simple and small guide to creating animations using the power of C# programming and the versatility of FFmpeg. I have been working on FFmpeg-related projects as a hobby for a long time. So I decided to write a book on FFmpeg. FFmpeg is a bigger software with many capabilities, and I am only covering a small subset in this book. I wrote this book intending to help fellow developers learn and develop this idea discussed in this book. I kept this book as small as possible and focused on delivering the core concepts to the users. Full source code of examples and projects is publicly available to download. So, let's embark on this journey together and unlock the potential of multimedia in your applications!

Happy coding!

Jayasankar S

Chapter 1

Getting Started

Animation is an illusion of movement created through a rapid succession of still images or frames. It is a technique used in filmmaking, video production, and multimedia design to bring inanimate objects or drawings to life. The human eye perceives them as continuous motion by quickly displaying slightly different Images. Daily we come across many animations in the form of cartoons, special effects in movies, colorful screensavers, games, advertisements, etc. In an animation video, you can see the object's shape changes, view angles changes, moving direction changes, speed changes, color changes, etc. Let's take the case of a cartoon video. A cartoon video contains cartoon characters, each comprising many basic shapes like triangles, Rectangles, Circles, Squares, lines, etc. From Image to Image, these shapes change to create an illusion of real live objects.

What steps should you follow to create an animation video from scratch? First, decide upon what animation you want to make. Draw the Images using the tool you are comfortable with, like a drawing tool or a programming language. Decide which part of the picture is moving. While drawing picture by picture, make the change. If you are creating a video with 25 FPS(frames per second), each second video consists of 25 Images. The difference happened in one second in the video distributed along these 25 Images. Once the pictures are created, you can convert them into video, and your animation is ready.

This book is for .Net developers who want to create animation videos or animation software using .Net code. A .Net programmer who knows basic programming can create animated videos or software using the topics discussed in this book. The fundamental question arises: how will you make a video using .Net? I am only creating Images using .Net. FFmpeg binaries convert these Images into videos and do other tasks like sound mixing, editing, splitting, merging, etc. Using .Net code, I am controlling what FFmpeg is doing. FFmpeg is an open-source library containing programs to handle video and audio. All the examples in this book are written in C# based on GDI+ and WPF.

The topics explained in this book are

- Downloading and setting up FFmpeg binaries.
- GDI+ and WPF basics.
- Basic FFmpeg commands to do video and audio editing.
- Creating pictures and converting them into videos.
- Mixing video and audio
- Merging multiple video and audio files.
- Creating simple 3D animation using WPF.
- Projects with complete code.

Download the source code of all projects/examples covered in this book at https://github.com/Jayasankar-S/CSharp-Animation-And-FFmpeg-Book

FFmpeg

FFmpeg is a free and open-source software project for handling multimedia files. It includes a command-line tool that I can use to create, edit, convert, record, and stream audio and video files in various formats. It supports popular formats like MP4, AVI, MOV, and less common formats. FFmpeg can record audio and video streams from various sources, including webcams, microphones, and screen capture software. FFmpeg can stream audio and video files over the internet or local network. It supports multiple streaming protocols, including HTTP, RTSP, and UDP. FFmpeg can be used in scripts and automated workflows to perform batch processing of media files. Overall, FFmpeg is a powerful and flexible tool for working with multimedia files and is widely used in the media industry and by developers working on media-related software projects. FF stands for Fast Forward, and MPEG stands for MPEG codex. I am not directly using FFmpeg code in the projects. Instead, use only binaries of FFmpeg, which can be run from a .Net code with options.

FFmpeg Binaries

FFmpeg binaries are compiled versions of the FFmpeg software that can be downloaded and installed on various operating systems, including Windows, Mac OS, and Linux. Binaries allow users to install and use FFmpeg without compiling the software from source code. FFmpeg binaries are three files, named ffmpeg.exe, ffplay.exe and ffprob.exe. The FFmpeg project provides official binaries for some platforms, but other organizations and individuals also provide compiled binaries. When downloading FFmpeg binaries, ensure they are from a trusted source and compatible with your operating system and hardware architecture. Using FFmpeg binaries typically involves downloading the appropriate package for your platform, extracting the files, and adding the FFmpeg executable path to your system's environment variable PATH to easily access it from the command line. Overall, using FFmpeg binaries can be a convenient way to start with FFmpeg and take advantage of its powerful features for working with multimedia files.

Initial Project Setup

Readers need basic .Net programming knowledge and experience with Visual Studio to understand this book. I used Visual Studio 2022 to create and test all examples and projects given in this book. These examples will work on lower versions also. To install visual studio, go to www.visualstudio.microsoft.com and download the Community, Professional, or Enterprise edition based on your subscription and go through the steps on the website to install it into your system. The Community edition is free for developers, students, and small businesses.

Using FFmpeg binaries

I need to download FFmpeg binaries to use it in my project. Below I am explaining the steps to download the binaries.

Go to www.ffmpeg.org, and you will see a Download button, as shown in Figure 1-1.

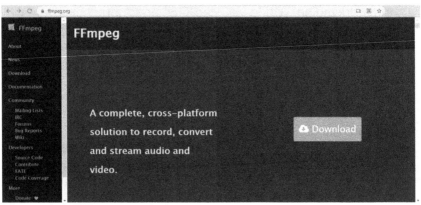

Figure 1-1. FFmpeg website

Click the Download button, which will take you to www.ffmpeg.org/download.html, as shown in Figure 1-2.

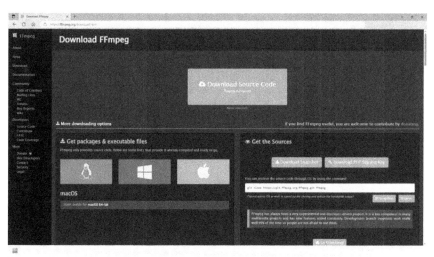

Figure 1-2. FFmpeg download page

Go to the "Get packages & executable files" section and click the Windows Icon button. Then the link to websites where Windows binaries are available will be displayed, as shown in Figure 1-3.

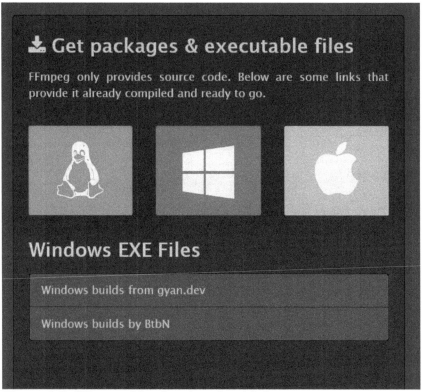

Figure 1-3. FFmpeg binaries download link

Figure 1.3 shows two links: "Windows builds from gyan.dev" and "Windows builds by BtbN". You can download binaries from any of these links. The first link, "Windows builds from gyan.dev", will take you to https://www.gyan.dev/ffmpeg/builds/, as shown in Figure 1-4.

Figure 1-4. gyan.dev download page

On this website, you can find links to download source code and binaries of different versions. Binaries come as a 7-zip compressed file with a .7z extension. I downloaded 'ffmpeg-release-essentials.zip' version 6.0. You can use free software like 7-zip to decompress the file. Once decompressed, you can see three files, ffmpeg.exe, ffplay.exe, and ffprob.exe, in the folder, as shown in Figure 1-5. These files are FFmpeg binaries used in the projects discussed later in this book.

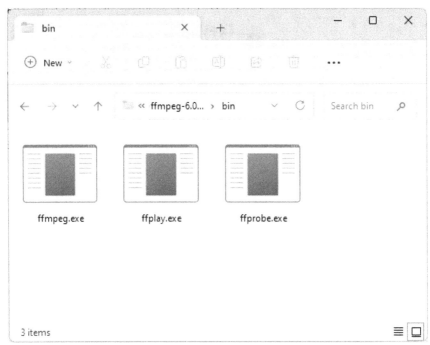

Figure 1-5. FFmpeg binaries

Coming back to the FFmpeg website, when you click on the other link, "Windows builds by BtbN," it goes to "https://github.com/BtbN/FFmpeg-Builds/releases" a GitHub repository, as shown in Figure 1-6. Different versions of FFmpeg binaries used on various platforms are available to download on this page. Download a win64 GPL zip file (for example, ffmpeg-n4.4-latest-win64-gpl-4.4.zip).

Figure 1-6. Windows builds by BtbN

Extract the Zip file, and in the bin folder, you can find three binary files, ffmpeg.exe, ffplay.exe, and ffprob.exe, as shown in Figure 1-5.

FFmpeg Commands and Command Prompt

You can use FFmpeg commands by copying FFmpeg binaries to the project's bin/Debug or bin/Release folder or the folder where your project binaries are present. Suppose you are distributing a project or an application. In that case, it is recommended to add FFmpeg binaries to the project folder or bin folder so that the client does not need to worry about adding FFmpeg binaries. In a development atmosphere, adding FFmpeg binaries to a common folder and setting the Environment variable PATH to make FFmpeg commands available in the command line is better.

To add FFmpeg commands to the command prompt, copy FFmpeg binaries to a common folder and add that path to the Environment variable PATH. Here are the steps.

1. Create a folder in C Drive named "FFmpeg" (or use any other folder). Copy FFmpeg binaries (ffmpeg.exe, ffplay.exe and ffprob.exe) to "C:\ffmpeg" folder.

2. Go to Windows Settings, and type "Environment variables" in the search box. A drop menu, as shown in Figure 1-7, appears. Select the "Edit the system environment variables" option. Then a window, as shown in Figure 1-8, appears.

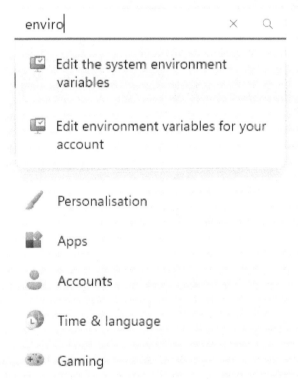

Figure 1-7. Settings

3. In this window (Figure 1-8), click the "Environment Variables" button at the bottom. Then another window, as shown in Figure 1-9, appears.

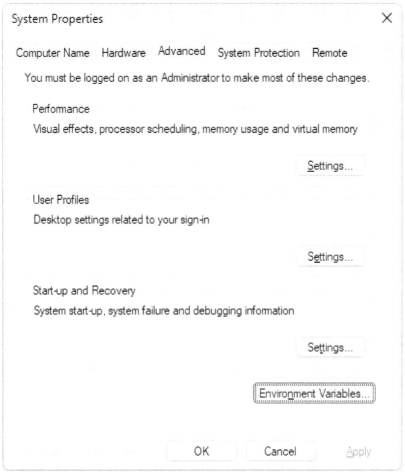

Figure 1-8. System Properties

Figure 1-9. Environment Variables

4. In the "System variables" section, click on the "Path" variable and click the "Edit" button. Then another window, as shown in Figure 1-10, appears.

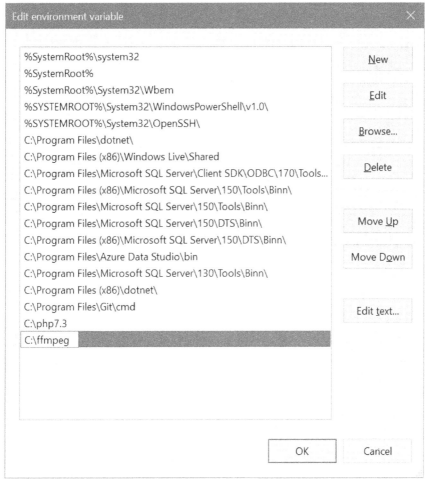

Figure 1-10. Adding new path

5. Click the "New" button, add the path of FFmpeg binary files as a new entry, and click the "OK" button to save and close.

Now the command prompt will recognize FFmpeg commands. To test it, open the command prompt and type 'ffmpeg -version". A result, as shown in Figure 1-11, will appear.

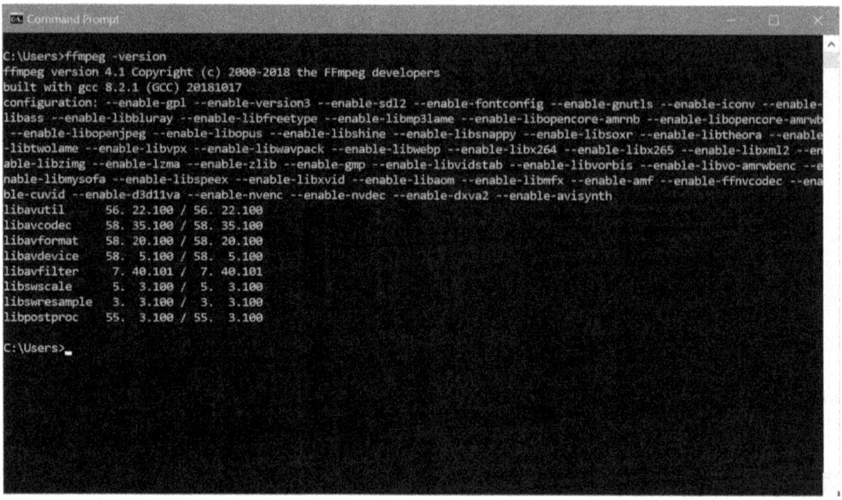

Figure 1-11. Running an FFmpeg command in Command Prompt

Setting up the .Net Application

In this section, I explain setting up a project in Visual Studio and adding FFmpeg binaries to the project's bin folder so you can use it from C# code. If you have already added FFmpeg commands to the command prompt, you do not need to add FFmpeg binaries to the bin folder. The same is the case of the WPF project, which I explained later in this chapter.

First, open Visual Studio, and a window like the one shown in Figure 1-12 will appear. Click the "Create a new Project" button.

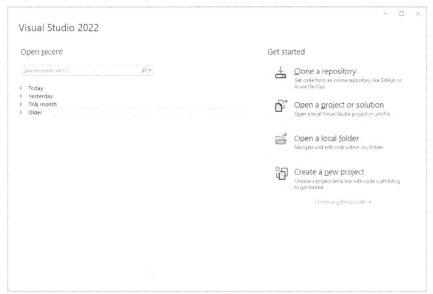

Figure 1-12. Visual Studio 2022

Then a "Create a new project" window will appear, as shown in Figure 1-13. In that, select "Console App (.Net Framework)" and click the "Next" button. You can create a desktop application also based on your requirement.

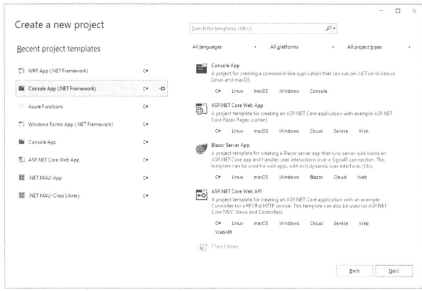

Figure 1-13 Create a new project.

In the next window (Figure 1-14), give the project's name, location, and .Net Framework version and click the "Next" button.

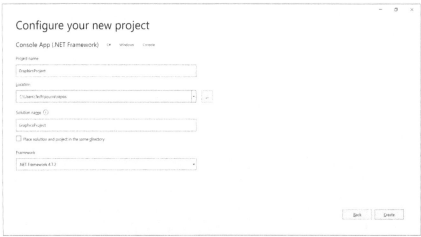

Figure 1-14. Project Configuration

Then a new project is created. In this project, you must add FFmpeg binaries to the bin folder. First, you need to build the project to get the bin folder created in the project. For that, click on the "Build" menu and select the "Build Solution" or "Build <project name>" option. A bin folder is created within your project folder, and your project binaries and related files are generated.

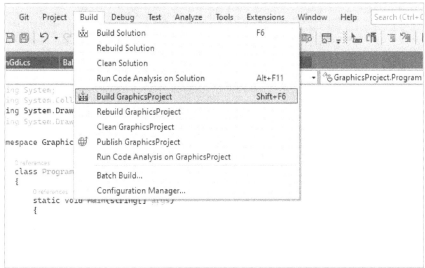

Figure 1-15. New project build

Once the bin folder is created, copy the FFmpeg binaries to your project's folder. It should be copied to the "bin\Debug" folder if you are running in debug mode, and it should be copied to the "bin\ Release" folder if you are running in release mode.

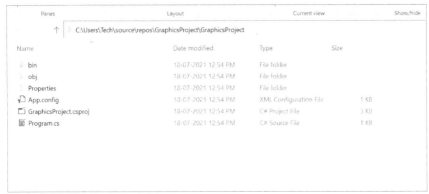

Figure 1-16. Project folder

Copy the FFmpeg binaries from the download location and paste them to the appropriate folder (Figure 1-17). Your project is now ready to run the FFmpeg commands from the project code.

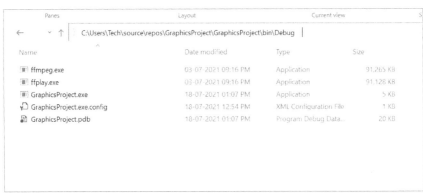

Figure 1-17. Project bin\Debug folder

Creating and Setting up the WPF Application

To create and set up a WPF application, open Visual Studio and click the "Create a new Project" button. Select "WPF App (.Net Framework)" in the new window and click Next.

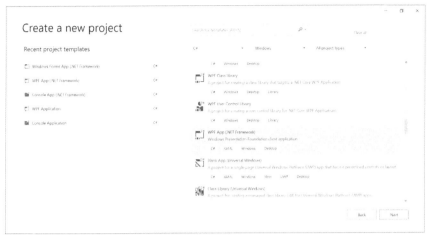

Figure 1-18. WPF new project

In the next window (Figure 1-18), give the project's name, location, and .Net Framework version and click the "Next" button.

Figure 1-19. WPF project Design and XAML

After the creation, build the project. Copy the FFmpeg binaries from the download location in the bin folder created. After that, go to "Properties" of the project, and, in the "Application" tab on the left side (Figure 1-20), set the output type to "Console Application." The reason for setting it as a Console application, even if it is not a Console application, is because, while running the project, the project opens a Console window along with the application window. A Console window is required because, while running the FFmpeg commands, many status messages will be generated from FFmpeg, and it will be updated in the Console. These messages are helpful for troubleshooting purposes and knowing the progress of the FFmpeg task.

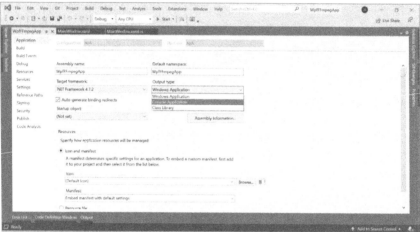

Figure 1-20. WPF project settings

Now the WPF project is ready to run the examples.

FFmpeg commands and their usage in projects are explained in the next chapter.

Chapter 2

Creating Animation

In this chapter, I am going through simple animation examples. Here I am explaining how to create sequential Images and how to mix these Images to create an animated full-HD video. What animation comes in the video depends on what I am drawing on the Images. What objects are moving, the moving objects' speed, the objects' color, etc., can be controlled while creating the Images. Once Images are created, I use FFmpeg commands to convert Images into video.

Download the source code of all projects/examples covered in this book at https://github.com/Jayasankar-S/CSharp-Animation-And-FFmpeg-Book

Creating Our First Project

I am starting with a simple animation project which outputs an MP4 video that contains a big grey Circle moving from left to right on white background. Initial setup of the project I explained in the first chapter. Ensure the FFmpeg binaries are copied to the bin folder or the environment variable PATH is updated with the path to FFmpeg binaries. Below is the full code of the project.

```
using System.Diagnostics;
using System.Drawing;
using System.Drawing.Drawing2D;
using System.IO;
```

```
Bitmap bmp = new Bitmap(1920, 1080);
Graphics g = Graphics.FromImage(bmp);
g.SmoothingMode = SmoothingMode.AntiAlias;

g.InterpolationMode =
    InterpolationMode.HighQualityBicubic;

int startX = 0;
int startY = 340;
int xIncrement = 10;

if (!Directory.Exists("ImageOutput"))
    Directory.CreateDirectory("ImageOutput");

if (!Directory.Exists("VideoOutput"))
    Directory.CreateDirectory("VideoOutput");

for (int i = 0; i < 125; i++)
{
    g.Clear(Color.White);

    g.FillEllipse(Brushes.Gray,
        new Rectangle(startX, startY, 400, 400));

    string imageName = "000000000" + i;

    imageName =
        imageName.Substring(imageName.Length - 6, 6);

    bmp.Save("ImageOutput\\" + imageName + ".png");
    Console.WriteLine("Created Image " + imageName);
    startX = startX + xIncrement;
}

CreateVideoFromImages(
    Path.GetFullPath("ImageOutput\\"),
    Path.GetFullPath("VideoOutput\\CircleMovingRight.mp4"));
```

First, a Bitmap object is created with a width of 1920 and a height of 1080, and a graphics object was created from that Bitmap, as shown below.

```
Bitmap bmp = new Bitmap(1920, 1080);
Graphics g = Graphics.FromImage(bmp);
```

The below code is added to draw objects of high quality.

```
g.SmoothingMode = SmoothingMode.AntiAlias;
g.InterpolationMode = InterpolationMode.HighQualityBicubic;
```

Next, I am creating 125 Images containing a grey Circle, whose position is increasing by 10 pixels Image by Image in the x direction, starting from 0. In the first Image, the Circle is drawn in the position (0, 340), which is the vertical middle position and horizontally on the left side of the Image. Image by Image, the Circle's position is changed by 10 pixels. I am using the 25 Frames per second(FPS) setting, which is FFmpeg's default value. It means 25 Images are required to create a one-second video. To change the frames per second value, I must pass that value as an option while running the FFmpeg command. Here using 125 Images, I am creating a 5-second video. The startX is starting x position of the Circle, startY is starting y position, and xIncrement is the increment value applied in each iteration.

```
int startX = 0;
int startY = 340;
int xIncrement = 10;
```

The following code ensures that folders required for storing the Images and video output are present. These folders are created inside the bin folder.

```
if (!Directory.Exists("ImageOutput"))
    Directory.CreateDirectory("ImageOutput");

if (!Directory.Exists("VideoOutput"))
    Directory.CreateDirectory("VideoOutput");
```

The following code creates 125 Images. Images are cleared with white color, erasing any previously drawn items. Next, a Circle is drawn in position (startX, startY) with a diameter 400. After drawing the Circle, these Images are saved to file as PNG Images using bmp.Save() method.

```
for (int i = 0; i < 125; i++)
{
    g.Clear(Color.White);
    g.FillEllipse(Brushes.Gray,
            new Rectangle(startX, startY, 400, 400));

    string imageName = "000000000" + i;

    imageName = imageName.Substring(
            imageName.Length - 6, 6);

    bmp.Save("ImageOutput\\" + imageName + ".png");
    startX = startX + xIncrement;
}
```

A very important thing to be noticed here is the file names used. File names should be a part of a sequence with a fixed length. Here file names used are "000000.png", "000001.png", "000002.png", "000003.png", "000004.png", "000005.png", etc. After creating these Images, the folder path is passed to FFmpeg to convert the Images in that folder to video. FFmpeg identifies these name patterns by using a regular expression. When I run the FFmpeg command, I have to pass a regular expression (in this case, "%06d.png") to FFmpeg as a command line option to filter the required Images and correctly arrange the Images in the video. Here the name of the Image file is created by the following code.

```
string imageName="000000000"+i;
imageName=imageName.Substring(imageName.Length-6,6);
```

This code will ensure that Image names follow a particular number sequence and are always in fixed length to match the regular expression. Images created in the ImageOutput folder are shown below in Figure 2-1.

Figure 2-1. Output Images

CreateVideoFromImages Method

Once the Image creation is completed, the CreateVideoFromImages method converts these Images to a video file. The CreateVideoFromImages method is the core part of our project, which interacts with FFmpeg binaries and converts Images to an Mp4 video file. In the CreateVideoFromImages method, the 'process.StartInfo.FileName' property is set with the application's name to run, which is the Windows command prompt in our case. Then 'process.StartInfo.Arguments' property is set with the arguments required to run in the command prompt, which is the FFmpeg command string. The code

```
Process process = new Process();
process.StartInfo.FileName = "cmd.exe";

process.StartInfo.Arguments = "/C " + " ffmpeg -i \"" +
    inputImagesfolder +
```

```
        "%06d.png\" -y -pix_fmt yuv420p  \""
        + videoOutputFile + "\" ";

process.StartInfo.UseShellExecute = false;
process.Start();
```

will run the FFmpeg command in the command prompt and convert the Images into Mp4 video. Below is the full code of the CreateVideoFromImages method.

```
public static void CreateVideoFromImages(
        string inputImagesfolder,
        string videoOutputFile)
{
    Process process = new Process();
    process.StartInfo.FileName = "cmd.exe";

    process.StartInfo.Arguments = "/C " + " ffmpeg -i \"" +
        inputImagesfolder +
        "%06d.png\" -y -pix_fmt yuv420p  \""
        + videoOutputFile + "\" ";

    process.StartInfo.UseShellExecute = false;
    process.Start();
    process.WaitForExit();

    int exitCode = process.ExitCode;
    if (exitCode == 0)
    {
        Console.WriteLine("Creating Video From" +
            " Images completed successfully!");
    }
    else
    {
        Console.WriteLine($"FFmpeg processing " +
            $"failed with exit code: {exitCode}");
    }
}
```

Incorrect Image names, incorrect input and output paths, unwanted spaces, and incorrect syntax can prevent FFmpeg from creating the video. When you run the project, the FFmpeg command runs in the command window, as shown in Figure 2-2, and at the end "CircleMovingRight.mp4" file is created in the "VideoOutput" folder.

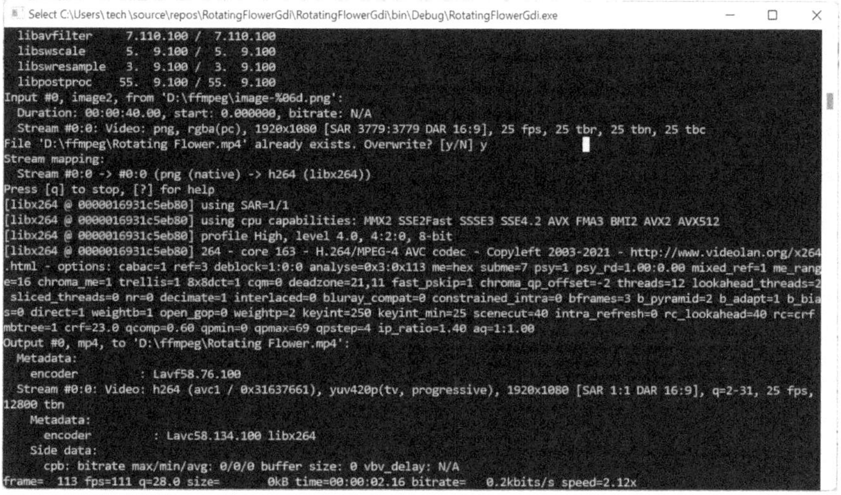

Figure 2-2. FFmpeg command executing

Moving a Circle Vertically downward
In this example, I am creating a video of the same Circle moving vertically downwards instead of from left to right. So to achieve the downward motion, I am keeping the startX constant and increasing startY Image by Image. Below is the code.

```
Bitmap bmp = new Bitmap(1920, 1080);
Graphics g = Graphics.FromImage(bmp);
g.SmoothingMode = SmoothingMode.AntiAlias;
g.InterpolationMode =
    InterpolationMode.HighQualityBicubic;

int startX = 760;
int startY = 0;
int yIncrement = 10;
```

```
if (!Directory.Exists("ImageOutput"))
    Directory.CreateDirectory("ImageOutput");

if (!Directory.Exists("VideoOutput"))
    Directory.CreateDirectory("VideoOutput");

for (int i = 0; i < 125; i++)
{
    g.Clear(Color.White);
    g.FillEllipse(Brushes.Gray,
        new Rectangle(startX, startY, 400, 400));

    string imageName = "000000000" + i;

    imageName =
        imageName.Substring(imageName.Length - 6, 6);

    bmp.Save("ImageOutput\\" + imageName + ".png");
    Console.WriteLine("Created Image " + imageName);
    startY = startY + yIncrement;
}

CreateVideoFromImages(
    Path.GetFullPath("ImageOutput\\"),
    Path.GetFullPath("VideoOutput\\CircleMovingDown.mp4"));
```

Images are created in the ImageOutput folder, as shown in Figure 2-3. FFmpeg uses these Images to create the video file "CircleMoveDown.mp4" in the VideoOutput folder.

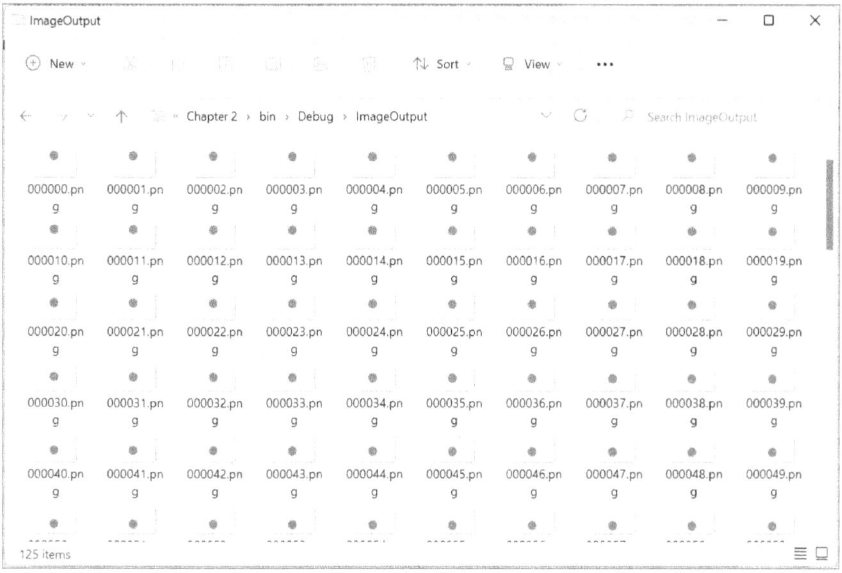

Figure 2-3. Output Images

Here startX is kept constant at 760, which is the horizontal middle of the Image, and startY is starting at 0, which is the top. StartY is incremented by 10 in each iteration. That means, Image by Image, the Y position of the Circle increases, and it moves down.

...

```
int startX = 760;
int startY = 0;
int yIncrement = 10;
```

...

```
for (int i = 0; i < 125; i++)
{
    ...

    g.FillEllipse(Brushes.Gray,
        new Rectangle(startX, startY, 400, 400));
    ...
    bmp.Save("ImageOutput\\" + imageName + ".png");
```

```
        startY = startY + yIncrement;
}
```

Circular Pie Animation

In the next example, I am creating a video of a circular Pie animation in which the video displays a Pie with a small sweep angle at first and, Image by Image, increases its sweep angle to 360 degrees, thus completing a full Circle.   So I am changing the above code like this.

```
Bitmap bmp = new Bitmap(1920, 1080);
Graphics g = Graphics.FromImage(bmp);
g.SmoothingMode = SmoothingMode.AntiAlias;

g.InterpolationMode =
    InterpolationMode.HighQualityBicubic;

int sweepAngle = 3;

if (!Directory.Exists("ImageOutput"))
    Directory.CreateDirectory("ImageOutput");

if (!Directory.Exists("VideoOutput"))
    Directory.CreateDirectory("VideoOutput");

for (int i = 0; i < 125; i++)
{
    g.Clear(Color.White);

    g.FillPie(Brushes.Gray,
        new Rectangle(760, 340, 400, 400), 0, sweepAngle);

    string imageName = "000000000" + i;

    imageName =
        imageName.Substring(imageName.Length - 6, 6);

    bmp.Save("ImageOutput\\" + imageName + ".png");
    Console.WriteLine("Created Image " + imageName);
```

```
    sweepAngle = sweepAngle + 3;
}

CreateVideoFromImages(
    Path.GetFullPath("ImageOutput\\"),
    Path.GetFullPath("VideoOutput\\CircleCompletion.mp4"));
```

Images are created in the ImageOutput folder, as shown in Figure 2-4. FFmpeg uses these Images to create the video file "CircleCompletion.mp4" in the "VideoOutput" folder.

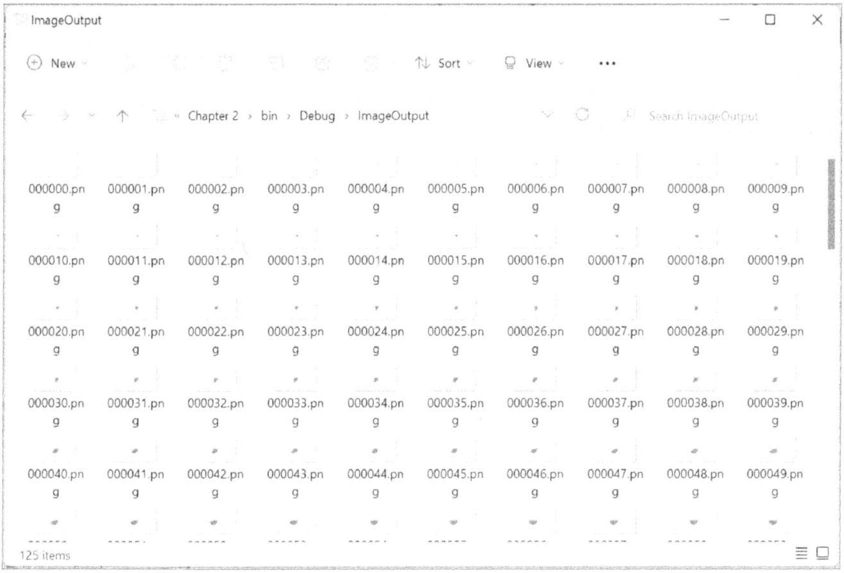

Figure 2-4. Output Images

First, a sweepAngle variable is declared with a value of 3 degrees. This sweepAngle variable is used in the FillPie method. At first, startAngle is 0 and sweepAngle 3, then Image by Image sweepAngle is increased by 3.

```
...
int sweepAngle = 3;
...
```

```
for (int i = 0; i < 125; i++)
{

    g.FillPie(Brushes.Gray,
        new Rectangle(760, 340, 400, 400), 0, sweepAngle);
    ...
    bmp.Save("ImageOutput\\" + imageName + ".png");
    sweepAngle = sweepAngle + 3;
}
```

FFmpeg and Images

In the above examples, I explained how to create a sequence of Images and how to convert those Images to a video file using the FFmpeg command. I can use whatever technology or any computer language to create those sequential Images and use the FFmpeg command to convert them to video. I do not need to call the FFmpeg command from the C# code. Instead, I can run those commands directly in the command prompt, which produces the same result.   The things that need to take care of are the FFmpeg command syntax, FFmpeg binary location, Image folder path, and output video file path. While running the FFmpeg command, special care should be taken about the position of double quotes, spaces, hyphens, etc. A dislocated space, a dislocated double, or a single quote can result in an error. More about FFmpeg commands are explained in the next chapter.

Chapter 3

FFmpeg

The FFmpeg project was started by Fabrice Bellard in 2000 and has since been developed by a group of volunteers. The tool has a vast network of developers and users working to enhance its features. It is suitable for personal use and is licensed under GNU Lesser General Public License 2.1+ or GNU General Public License 2+, depending on the selected options. It's always a good idea to consult with a legal professional or seek expert advice to ensure that you are fully compliant with the licensing requirements when using FFmpeg in your commercial applications.

FFmpeg is a powerful multimedia framework that can be used to convert, edit, record, encode, decode, transcode, mux, demux, add or remove frames, apply filters, change the playback speed, resize and crop videos, add watermarks, create time-lapse videos or record your screen recording video from a webcam or screen capture, streaming live video to YouTube or Facebook, and play almost any type of video or audio file. It supports various codecs and formats, including popular ones like MP4, AVI, MOV, FLV, and WMV. FFmpeg supports a wide range of codecs and formats, and it is also the foundation for many popular media players such as VLC and Mplayer. Many companies and organizations use it to handle their video and audio processing needs.

In this chapter, I explain how to use FFmpeg binaries to create, convert, edit, mix, and extract audio and video files. Here I am explaining only a small subset of FFmpeg features related to audio and video editing.

Download the source code of all projects/examples covered in this book at https://github.com/Jayasankar-S/CSharp-Animation-And-FFmpeg-Book

Converting Images to Video

The CreateVideoFromImages method, given below, converts Images to video. I can convert Images to any video format that FFmpeg supports. The only requirement is that the appropriate codec be available in the system. The CreateVideoFromImages method takes three arguments: the frame rate, the folder path where the Images are available and the output video file path. Below is the full code of the CreateVideoFromImages method.

```
public static void CreateVideoFromImages(
    int frameRate,
    string inputImagesfolder,
    string videoOutputFile)
{
    Process process = new Process();
    process.StartInfo.FileName = "cmd.exe";

    process.StartInfo.Arguments = "/C " + " ffmpeg -i \"" +
        inputImagesfolder +
        "%06d.png\" -r "+ frameRate + " -y -pix_fmt yuv420p \""
        + videoOutputFile + "\" ";

    process.StartInfo.UseShellExecute = false;
    process.Start();
    process.WaitForExit();

    int exitCode = process.ExitCode;

    if (exitCode == 0)
    {
        Console.WriteLine("Creating Video From" +
            " Images completed successfully!");
    }
}
```

```
    else
    {
        Console.WriteLine($"FFmpeg processing " +
            $"failed with exit code: {exitCode}");
    }
}
```

Here I am running the FFmpeg command from the command prompt. To run from the command prompt, I need first to start the command prompt. I can use the System.Diagnostics.Process and System.Diagnostics.ProcessStartInfo classes to accomplish this.

```
Process process = new Process();
process.StartInfo.FileName = "cmd.exe";

process.StartInfo.Arguments = "/C " + " ffmpeg -i \"" +
    inputImagesfolder +
    "%06d.png\" -r "+ frameRate + " -y -pix_fmt yuv420p \""
    + videoOutputFile + "\" ";

    process.StartInfo.UseShellExecute = false;
    process.Start();
    process.WaitForExit();
```

ProcessStartInfo class takes the application's name to run as the first parameter and arguments as the second parameter. I need to run "cmd.exe" and pass the FFmpeg command as the argument. FFmpeg command runs with options to produce the desired result.

Let's look into the details of the FFmpeg command. The arguments string starts with /C, which is not an option of FFmpeg but is an option related to cmd.exe to close the command window after the execution of the command. Using the /C option, the command window executes the task, closes itself, and moves to the next line of code. On the other hand, if I use option /K, the command window will not be closed after execution. Keeping the window open will help us see the output messages from the FFmpeg. This will be helpful in case of diagnostic purposes, where

I can read any error messages and correct them accordingly. Use the /K option only in case of an error.

After the /C, the FFmpeg command section starts. The remaining part of the argument is the FFmpeg command and its options. Look into the below part.

" ffmpeg -y -i \"" + inputImageFolder + "%06d.png\"

This part runs the ffmpeg.exe from the command prompt. The "-y" option confirms the output file can be overwritten if already present in the output path, and there is no need to ask for confirmation. FFmpeg will ask permission to overwrite the file if I do not add the "-y" option.

The "-i" option marks the input file or files. In our case, I am giving a path to the Images folder. The "-i" option should be present before each input file/folder path. A regular expression follows the folder path to identify Images and their order. The expression "%06d.png" means the file name should end with ".png," and the file name should contain six digits, either zero or other. So input Images should follow a name pattern like arithmetic progression, and six digits should be present. So to keep the six-digit constraint, I need to add leading zeros if required. The Image names I should give, as per the above rule, will be "000000.png", "000001.png",   "000002.png",   "000003.png",   "000004.png", "000005.png",   "000006.png" etc. Instead of "%06d.png", I can use "%05d.png," "%04d.png," or "image-%04d.png" or any other name pattern which fits sequential file names.

Expression	Sample filenames
%05d.png	00000.png, 00001.png, 00002.png etc
%04d.png	0000.png, 0001.png, 0002.png etc
image-%04d.png	image-0000.png, image-0001.png, image-0002.png etc.

FFmpeg will not create a video if the Image names and the regular expression is not matching and will result in an error.

The next options in the arguments string are related frame rate.

-r "+ frameRate

Frame rate is the measurement of how quickly a number of frames appears within a second. '-r 30' sets the output frame rate to 30 frames per second (FPS).

The next options in the arguments string are related to the output format and the output file path.

-pix_fmt yuv420p \"" + videoOutputFile + "\"

The -pix_fmt yuv420p is the chroma subsampling scheme, and the p stands for planar, not progressive. FFmpeg will automatically use the appropriate codec to match the output file extension. An output file name with ".Mp4" extension uses mpeg4 codec even if it is not explicitly specified.

Example :

```
Bitmap bmp = new Bitmap(1920, 1080);
Graphics g = Graphics.FromImage(bmp);
g.SmoothingMode = SmoothingMode.AntiAlias;

g.InterpolationMode =
    InterpolationMode.HighQualityBicubic;

int startX = 0;
int startY = 340;
int xIncrement = 10;


for (int i = 0; i < 125; i++)
{
    g.Clear(Color.White);

    g.FillEllipse(Brushes.Gray,
```

```
        new Rectangle(startX, startY, 400, 400));

    string imageName = "000000000" + i;

    imageName =
        imageName.Substring(imageName.Length - 6, 6);

    bmp.Save("ImageOutput\\" + imageName + ".png");
    Console.WriteLine("Created image " + imageName);
    startX = startX + xIncrement;
}

CreateVideoFromImages(
    Path.GetFullPath("ImageOutput\\"),
    Path.GetFullPath("VideoOutput\\Output.mp4"));
```

Converting Video File from Mpeg4 to Mpeg1 Format

In this section, I explain converting Mpeg4 video to Mpeg1 format. The method ConvertFromMp4ToMpeg1 method converts an Mp4 video file to Mpeg1 format. The method takes two parameters, One is the input video file path, and the other one is the output video file path. Below is the full code of the ConvertFromMp4ToMpeg1 method.

```
public static void ConvertFromMp4ToMpeg1(
    string inputVideoFilePath,
    string outputVideoFilePath)
{

    Process process = new Process();
    process.StartInfo.FileName = "cmd.exe";

    process.StartInfo.Arguments = "/C " + " ffmpeg  -y -i " +
        inputVideoFilePath +
        " -f  mpeg1video -acodec copy  " +
        outputVideoFilePath;
```

```
process.StartInfo.UseShellExecute = false;
process.Start();
process.WaitForExit();

int exitCode = process.ExitCode;

if (exitCode == 0)
{
    Console.WriteLine("Conversion " +
        " completed successfully!");
}
else
{
    Console.WriteLine($"FFmpeg processing " +
        $"failed with exit code: {exitCode}");
}
}
```

Look at the arguments section.

```
process.StartInfo.Arguments = "/C " + " ffmpeg -y -i " +
    inputVideoFilePath +
    " -f mpeg1video -acodec copy " +
    outputVideoFilePath;
```

The option " -f mpeg1video " forces the mpeg1video codec to convert from Mpeg4 to Mpeg1 format. The option "-a codec" specifies the audio codec to create the output file. Here " -a codec copy " copies the audio stream from the input file to the output file without making any changes.

Example :
```
ConvertFromMp4ToMpeg1(
"VideoOutput\\Input.mp4",
"VideoOutput\\Output.mpeg");
```

Creating 4K Video from Images

The Create4KVideoFromImages method creates a 4K video from images. The Create4KVideoFromImages method takes three arguments: the frame rate, the folder path where the Images are available, and the output video file path. Below is the full code of the Create4KVideoFromImages method.

```csharp
public static void Create4KVideoFromImages(
    int frameRate,
    string inputImagesfolder,
    string videoOutputFile)
{
    Process process = new Process();
    process.StartInfo.FileName = "cmd.exe";

    process.StartInfo.Arguments = "/C " + " ffmpeg -i \"" +
        inputImagesfolder +
        "%06d.png\"  -r "+ frameRate +
        " -pattern_type glob "+
        " -s 3840x2160 "+
        "-c:v libx264 -preset slow "+
        " -crf 18 \""
        + videoOutputFile + "\" ";

    process.StartInfo.UseShellExecute = false;
    process.Start();
    process.WaitForExit();

    int exitCode = process.ExitCode;

    if (exitCode == 0)
    {
        Console.WriteLine("Conversion " +
            " completed successfully!");
    }
    else
    {
        Console.WriteLine($"FFmpeg processing " +
            $"failed with exit code: {exitCode}");
```

```
    }
}
```

The option '-r + frameRate' sets the frame rate (FPS). Option '-s 3840x2160' sets the output resolution to 3840x2160, the standard 4K resolution. Option '-c:v libx264' selects the x264 video codec for encoding. x264 is a widely used and efficient video codec. Option '-crf 18' sets the Constant Rate Factor (CRF) for video quality. Lower values result in higher quality but larger file sizes. 18-28 is typically considered a good range, where 18 is visually lossless or nearly lossless.

Example :

```
Bitmap bmp = new Bitmap(3840, 2160);
Graphics g = Graphics.FromImage(bmp);
g.SmoothingMode = SmoothingMode.AntiAlias;

g.InterpolationMode =
    InterpolationMode.HighQualityBicubic;

int startX = 0;
int startY = 1080;
int xIncrement = 10;


for (int i = 0; i < 1000; i++)
{
    g.Clear(Color.White);

    g.FillEllipse(Brushes.Gray,
        new Rectangle(startX, startY, 400, 400));

    string imageName = "000000000" + i;

    imageName =
        imageName.Substring(imageName.Length - 6, 6);

    bmp.Save("ImageOutput\\" + imageName + ".png");
    Console.WriteLine("Created image " + imageName);
    startX = startX + xIncrement;
```

```
}

Create4KVideoFromImages(25,
        Path.GetFullPath("ImageOutput\\"),
        Path.GetFullPath("VideoOutput\\Output.mp4"));
```

Converting Mp4 Video to Mkv format

The ConvertFromMp4ToMkv method converts an Mp4 video file to an Mkv video file. The method takes two parameters, One is the input video file path, and the other one is the output video file path. Below is the full code of the ConvertFromMp4ToMkv method.

```
public static void ConvertFromMp4ToMkv(
    string inputVideoFilePath,
    string outputVideoFilePath)
{

    Process process = new Process();
    process.StartInfo.FileName = "cmd.exe";

    process.StartInfo.Arguments = "/C " + " ffmpeg  -y -i " +
        inputVideoFilePath +
        " -codec:v libx264 -codec:a libmp3lame  " +
        outputVideoFilePath;

    process.StartInfo.UseShellExecute = false;
    process.Start();
    process.WaitForExit();

    int exitCode = process.ExitCode;

    if (exitCode == 0)
    {
        Console.WriteLine(""Conversion " +
            " completed successfully!"");
    }
    else
```

```
    {
        Console.WriteLine($"FFmpeg processing " +
            $"failed with exit code: {exitCode}");
    }
}
```

The option '-codec:v libx264' sets the video codec to libx264, an open-source H.264 encoder. The option '-codec:a libmp3lame' sets the audio codec to libmp3lame, an MP3 audio encoder.

```
Example :
 ConvertFromMp4ToMkv(
        "VideoOutput\\Input.mp4",
        "VideoOutput\\Output.mkv");
```

Merging Two Videos

The MergeVideo method merges two videos without audio. The MergeVideo method takes three parameters, the first two parameters are the input video file paths, and the last one is the output video file path. Below is the full code of the MergeVideo method.

```
public static void MergeVideo(
    string inputVideoFilePath1,
    string inputVideoFilePath2,
    string outputVideoFilePath)
{
    Process process = new Process();
    process.StartInfo.FileName = "cmd.exe";

    process.StartInfo.Arguments = "/C " + " ffmpeg -y -i " +
        inputVideoFilePath1 + " -i " + inputVideoFilePath2 +
        " -filter_complex \"[0:v] [1:v] " +
        "concat=n=2:v=1 [v] \" -map \"[v]\" \"" +
        outputVideoFilePath + "\" ";

    process.StartInfo.UseShellExecute = false;
    process.Start();
    process.WaitForExit();
```

```
        int exitCode = process.ExitCode;
        if (exitCode == 0)
        {
            Console.WriteLine("Merging " +
                " completed successfully!");
        }
        else
        {
            Console.WriteLine($"FFmpeg processing " +
                $"failed with exit code: {exitCode}");
        }
    }
```

FFmpeg -filter_complex option is used to select the streams precisely. Here [0:v] represents the video stream of the first video, and [1:v] represents the video stream of the second video. So only the first and second video stream is selected and concat using the contact option.

```
" -filter_complex \"[0:v] [1:v] concat=n=2:v=1 [v] \" -map \"[v]\"  \""
+
        outputVideoFilePath +"\" ";
```

The option concat=n=2:v=1 [v] means concat two videos to one, and [v] represents the output video. The -map \"[v]\" options maps that merged video to the output file. Here I deliberately avoided audio. The audio stream will be ignored if present in any of the input files.

Example :
MergeVideo(
"VideoOutput\\Input1.mp4",
"VideoOutput\\Input2.mp4",
"VideoOutput\\Output.mp4");

Merging Two Videos along with the Audio

The MergeVideoWithAudio merges two videos into one, along with the audio. MergeVideoWithAudio takes three parameters, the first two parameters are the input video file paths, and the last one is the output video file path. Below is the full code of the MergeVideoWithAudio method.

```csharp
public static void MergeVideoWithAudio(
    string inputVideoFilePath1,
    string inputVideoFilePath2,
    string outputVideoFilePath)
{
    Process process = new Process();
    process.StartInfo.FileName = "cmd.exe";

    process.StartInfo.Arguments = "/C " + " ffmpeg -y -i " +
        inputVideoFilePath1 + " -i " + inputVideoFilePath2 +
        " -filter_complex \"[0:v] [0:a] [1:v] [1:a] " +
        "concat=n=2:v=1:a=1 " +
        "[v] [a]\" -map \"[v]\" -map \"[a]\" \"" +
        outputVideoFilePath + "\" ";

    process.StartInfo.UseShellExecute = false;
    process.Start();
    process.WaitForExit();

    int exitCode = process.ExitCode;
    if (exitCode == 0)
    {
        Console.WriteLine("Merging " +
          " completed successfully!");
    }
    else
    {
        Console.WriteLine($"FFmpeg processing " +
          $"failed with exit code: {exitCode}");
    }
}
```

```
}
```

Like in the previous example, FFmpeg -filter_complex option is used to select the streams precisely. Here [0:v] represents the video stream of the first video, [0:a] represents the audio stream of the first video, [1:v] represents the video stream of the second video, and [1:a] represents the audio stream of the second video. So video streams along with audio streams are selected for concatenation.

```
" -filter_complex \"[0:v] [0:a] [1:v] [1:a] concat=n=2:v=1:a=1 [v] [a]\"
-map \"[v]\" -map \"[a]\" \"" +  outputVideoFilePath + "\" ";
```

The option concat=n=2:v=1:a=1 [v][a] means concat two videos to one, and [v] and [a] represent the concat video and audio, respectively. The -map \"[v]\" and -map \"[a]\" options maps merge video and audio to the output file.

Example :
```
 MergeVideoWithAudio(
 "VideoOutput\\Input1.mp4",
 "VideoOutput\\Input2.mp4",
 "VideoOutput\\Output.mp4");
```

Merging two Audio Files

The MergeAudio method merges two audio into one audio file. MergeAudio takes three parameters, the first two parameters are the input audio file paths, and the last one is the output audio file path.

Below is the full code of the MergeAudio method.

```
public static void MergeAudio(
    string inputAudioFilePath1,
    string inputAudioFilePath2,
    string outputAudioFilePath)
{
```

```
Process process = new Process();
process.StartInfo.FileName = "cmd.exe";

process.StartInfo.Arguments = "/C " + " ffmpeg -y -i " +
    inputAudioFilePath1 +
    " -i " + inputAudioFilePath2 +
    " -filter_complex \"[0:a] [1:a] " +
    "concat=n=2:v=0:a=1 [a]\" -map \"[a]\" \"" +
    outputAudioFilePath + "\" ";

process.StartInfo.UseShellExecute = false;
process.Start();
process.WaitForExit();

int exitCode = process.ExitCode;
if (exitCode == 0)
{
    Console.WriteLine("Merging " +
        " completed successfully!");
}
else
{
    Console.WriteLine($"FFmpeg processing " +
        $"failed with exit code: {exitCode}");
}
}
```

Here [0:a] represents the audio stream of the first audio file, and [1:a] represents the audio stream of the second audio file. So audio streams are selected for concatenation.

" -filter_complex \"[0:a] [1:a] concat=n=2:v=0:a=1 [a]\" -map \"[a]\" \"" + outputAudioFilePath + "\" "

The option concat=n=2:v=0:a=1 [a] means concat two audios to one, and [a] represents the concat audio stream. The -map \"[a]\" options maps that merge audio to the output file.

Example :
 MergeAudio("Dream_It.mp3","Gully_Dreams.mp3",
"VideoOutput\\merged.mp3");

Mixing Audio and Video

The MixAudioAndVideo method mixes an audio file and a video file to create a video file output containing both video and audio streams. MixAudioAndVideo takes four parameters. The first is the time string in the format "hh:mm:ss." This time string specifies when the audio starts while playing the video. For example, if the time string "00:00:06" is given, the audio starts at the 6th second. The second parameter is the input video file path, and the third is the audio file path. The fourth parameter is the output video file path.

```
public static void MixAudioAndVideo(
    string timestring,
    string inputVideoFilePath,
    string inputAudioFilePath,
    string outputVideoFilePath)
{
    Process process = new Process();
    process.StartInfo.FileName = "cmd.exe";

    process.StartInfo.Arguments = "/C " + " ffmpeg -y  -i \"" +
        inputVideoFilePath +
        "\" -itsoffset " + timestring + " -i \"" +
        inputAudioFilePath +
        "\" -map 0:0 -map 1:0 -c:v copy  -async 1  \"" +
        outputVideoFilePath + "\" ";

    process.StartInfo.UseShellExecute = false;
    process.Start();
    process.WaitForExit();

    int exitCode = process.ExitCode;

    if (exitCode == 0)
```

```
    {
        Console.WriteLine("Mixing " +
            " completed successfully!");
    }
    else
    {
        Console.WriteLine($"FFmpeg processing " +
            $"failed with exit code: {exitCode}");
    }

}
```

Here FFmpeg takes two input files, inputVideoFilePath, and inputAudioFilePath, marked with the -i option. The -itsoffset " + timestring + " option specifies the time offset when the audio starts in the video file. -map 0:0 -map 1:0 means the first stream of the video file and the first stream of the second audio file. The -c:v copy copies the audio file to the video file output.

Example :
MixAudioAndVideo("00:00:00", "VideoOutput\\Input1.mp4", "VideoOutput\\Input2.mp3", "VideoOutput\\Output.mp4");

Cutting an Audio

CutAudio methods cut an audio segment from an audio file and save it to a new file. CutAudio method takes four parameters, the first one is the input audio file path, and the second one is the output audio file path. The third parameter is the starting time of the audio, where the new audio should start, and the fourth parameter is the time length of the output audio from the starting point.

```
  public static void CutAudio(
    string inputAudioFilePath,
    string outputAudioFilePath,
    int startPositionInSeconds,
    int durationInSeconds)
{
```

```
    Process process = new Process();
    process.StartInfo.FileName = "cmd.exe";

    process.StartInfo.Arguments = "/C " + " ffmpeg -y -ss " +
        startPositionInSeconds +
        " -t " + durationInSeconds + " -i \"" +
        inputAudioFilePath +
        "\" -acodec copy \"" + outputAudioFilePath + "\" ";

    process.StartInfo.UseShellExecute = false;
    process.Start();
    process.WaitForExit();

    int exitCode = process.ExitCode;

    if (exitCode == 0)
    {
        Console.WriteLine("Audio cutting " +
            " completed successfully!");
    }
    else
    {
        Console.WriteLine($"FFmpeg processing " +
            $"failed with exit code: {exitCode}");
    }
}
```

The "-ss + startPositionInSeconds" specifies the start position, which means where the new audio starts. The format of the time is in seconds. For example, -ss 12 starts the output audio in the 12th second of the input audio file. The " -t " + durationInSeconds specifies the duration of the output audio file.

Example :
CutAudio("Gully_Dreams.mp3", "VideoOutput\\cut2.mp3", 0, 5);

Cutting a Video

The CutVideo method cuts a video segment from a video file and saves it to a new file. The CutVideo method takes four parameters, the first one is the input video file path, and the second one is the output video file path. The third parameter is the starting time of the video, where the new video should start, and the fourth parameter is the time length of the output video from the starting point.

```
public static void CutVideo(
    string inputVideoFilePath,
    string outputVideoFilePath,
    int startPositionInSeconds,
    int durationInSeconds)
{

    Process process = new Process();
    process.StartInfo.FileName = "cmd.exe";

    process.StartInfo.Arguments = "/C " +
        " ffmpeg -y -ss " +
        startPositionInSeconds +
        " -t " + durationInSeconds + " -i \"" +
        inputVideoFilePath +
        "\" \"" + outputVideoFilePath + "\" ";

    process.StartInfo.UseShellExecute = false;
    process.Start();
    process.WaitForExit();

    int exitCode = process.ExitCode;

    if (exitCode == 0)
    {
        Console.WriteLine("Video cutting " +
            " completed successfully!");
    }
    else
    {
```

```
        Console.WriteLine($"FFmpeg processing " +
            $"failed with exit code: {exitCode}");
    }
}
```

The "-ss + startPositionInSeconds" specifies the start position, which means where the new video starts. The format of the time is in seconds. For example, -ss 12 starts the output video in the 12th second of the input file. The   " -t " + durationInSeconds specifies the duration of the output video file.

Example :
CutVideo("VideoOutput\\Input.mp4", "VideoOutput\\Output.mp4", 3, 5);

Getting Images From Video

The ConvertToImages method takes a video file path as a parameter and outputs all the frames in that video as Images. ConvertToImages takes two parameters, one is the input video file path, and the second one is the folder path where the output Images are saved.

```
public static void ConvertToImages(
    string inputVideoFilePath,
    string outputFolder)
{
    Process process = new Process();
    process.StartInfo.FileName = "cmd.exe";

    process.StartInfo.Arguments = "/C " +
        " ffmpeg -y -i " +
        inputVideoFilePath +
        " -vcodec png  " +
        outputFolder + "%06d.png ";

    process.StartInfo.UseShellExecute = false;
    process.Start();
    process.WaitForExit();
```

```
    int exitCode = process.ExitCode;

    if (exitCode == 0)
    {
        Console.WriteLine("Video to image conversion " +
            " completed successfully!");
    }
    else
    {
        Console.WriteLine($"FFmpeg processing " +
            $"failed with exit code: {exitCode}");
    }
}
```

The " -vcodec png " + outputFolder + "%06d.png " option converts the video file frames to Images in png format and saves them to the outputFolder. Images follow the name pattern specified by the regular expression "%06d.png". Here Images created will have names like "000000.png", "000001.png", "000002.png", "000003.png", "000004.png", "000005.png", "000006.png" etc. The file name has a .png extension and contains six digits as specified by the regular expression.

Example :
ConvertToImages("VideoOutput\\Input.mp4",
"ExtractedImages\\");

Extracting audio from a Video file

The ExtractAudioFromVideoFile method extracts the audio stream from the video file and saves it as an audio file. The method takes two parameters, the first one is the input video file, which contains the audio, and the second parameter is the output audio file path.

```
public static void ExtractAudioFromVideoFile(
    string inputVideoFilePath,
    string outputFilePath)
{
    Process process = new Process();
```

```
process.StartInfo.FileName = "cmd.exe";

process.StartInfo.Arguments = "/C " + " ffmpeg -y -i " +
    inputVideoFilePath +
    " -filter_complex \"[0:a]  " +
    "concat=n=1:v=0:a=1 [a]\" -map \"[a]\" \"" +
    outputFilePath + "\" ";

process.StartInfo.UseShellExecute = false;
process.Start();
process.WaitForExit();

int exitCode = process.ExitCode;

if (exitCode == 0)
{
    Console.WriteLine("Audio extraction " +
        " completed successfully!");
}
else
{
    Console.WriteLine($"FFmpeg processing " +
        $"failed with exit code: {exitCode}");
}
}
```

Here I am using FFmpeg -filter_complex option to select the stream. [0:a] represents the audio stream of the video. So only the audio stream is selected as the output.

```
" -filter_complex \"[0:a]  concat=n=1:v=0:a=1 [a]\" -map \"[a]\" \"" +
outputFilePath + "\" ";
```

The option concat=n=1:v=0:a=1 [a] means to select only the audio stream and avoid the video stream, and [a] represents the audio stream. The -map \"[a]\" option maps that audio stream from the video to the output file.

Example :
ExtractAudioFromVideoFile(

"VideoOutput\\Input.mp4",
"VideoOutput\\Output.mp3");

Resizing a Video

The ResizeVideo method changes the frame width and frame height of a video. The method takes four parameters, and One is the input video file path, second, is the output video file path, third is the new frame width, fourth is the new frame height. Below is the full code of the ResizeVideo method.

```
public static void ResizeVideo(
 string inputVideoFilePath,
 string outputVideoFilePath,
 int width,int height)
{

   Process process = new Process();
   process.StartInfo.FileName = "cmd.exe";

   process.StartInfo.Arguments = "/C " + " ffmpeg  -y -i " +
      inputVideoFilePath +
      " -vf scale="+ width + "x"+ height + ",setsar=1 " +
      outputVideoFilePath;

   process.StartInfo.UseShellExecute = false;
   process.Start();
   process.WaitForExit();

   int exitCode = process.ExitCode;

   if (exitCode == 0)
   {
      Console.WriteLine("Video resizing " +
         " completed successfully!");
   }
   else
   {
      Console.WriteLine($"FFmpeg processing " +
```

```
        $"failed with exit code: {exitCode}");
    }
}
```

Here the option ' -vf scale= widthxheight ' is the video filter to perform scaling. This option Replaces width and height with the desired width and height values for the output video. The setsar=1 filter in your FFmpeg command ensures that the pixel aspect ratio is set to 1, which helps maintain the correct display aspect ratio during playback.

Example :
```
ResizeVideo(
        "VideoOutput\\Input.mp4",
        "VideoOutput\\Output.mp4",300,500);
```

Creating Silent Audio

Silent audio is required when I create projects involving audio mixing. Sometimes, silent audio is needed with specific time intervals to fill the gaps between two audios. The CreateSilence method creates silent audio of specific time intervals in mp3 format and saves it to a file. The method takes two parameters, the first one is the audio output file path, and the second one is the length of the audio output in seconds.

```
public static void CreateSilence(
    string filePath,
    int seconds)
{
    Process process = new Process();
    process.StartInfo.FileName = "cmd.exe";

    process.StartInfo.Arguments = "/C " + " ffmpeg -y -f " +
        "lavfi -i anullsrc=r=24000:cl=mono -t " +
        seconds + " -b:a 32k " +
        "-ss 00:00:00 -acodec libmp3lame \"" +
        filePath + "\" ";

    process.StartInfo.UseShellExecute = false;
```

```csharp
    process.Start();
    process.WaitForExit();

    int exitCode = process.ExitCode;

    if (exitCode == 0)
    {
        Console.WriteLine("Silent audio" +
            " created successfully!");
    }
    else
    {
        Console.WriteLine($"FFmpeg processing " +
            $"failed with exit code: {exitCode}");
    }
}
```

Here option -f "lavfi -i anullsrc=r=24000:cl=mono" specifies the input format as a lavfi filter, specifically anullsrc. lavfi is a demuxer in FFmpeg that stands for "libavfilter input." It is used to input data from libavfilter, FFmpeg's filtering system. The lavfi demuxer allows you to use various audio and video filter chains as input sources for FFmpeg.The anullsrc is a lavfi filter in FFmpeg that generates silent audio. The option r=24000 sets the sample rate to 24000 Hz, cl=mono specifies a mono channel, -t seconds specifies the duration of the output audio file in seconds, -b:a 32k specifies the audio bitrate to 32 kbps, -ss 00:00:00 specifies the starting position of the input audio, -acodec libmp3lame specifies the audio codec to use for encoding the output file. libmp3lame is an FFmpeg encoder that utilizes the LAME MP3 library for encoding audio into the MP3 format.

Example :
CreateSilence("VideoOutput\\silence.mp4", 20);

Troubleshooting FFmpeg commands

When working with FFmpeg commands, you may encounter issues or errors. In the above methods, if any methods fail, we need to read the error messages to find the reason for failing. As per the current setting command window closes immediately in case of an error, and we cannot see the error messages. Change the /C option in the command argument to /K to get the error messages.

For example, change the below code.

```
process.StartInfo.Arguments = "/C " + " ffmpeg  -y -i " +
    inputVideoFilePath +
    " -vf scale="+ width + "x"+ height + ",setsar=1 " +
    outputVideoFilePath;
```

to

```
process.StartInfo.Arguments = "/K " + " ffmpeg  -y -i " +
    inputVideoFilePath +
    " -vf scale="+ width + "x"+ height + ",setsar=1 " +
    outputVideoFilePath;
```

This change will stop the execution after executing the command, and error messages, if any, will be displayed. Once issues are corrected, you can change it back to the /C option.

Ensure that FFmpeg is properly installed on your system and accessible from the command line. You can verify this by running the ffmpeg -version in the command prompt or terminal, which should display the FFmpeg version information. Double-check the paths to your input and output files. Make sure they are correct, including the correct file extensions. Also, ensure you have the necessary read and write permissions for the specified file locations. If your file paths or filenames contain spaces or special characters, you may need to enclose them in quotation marks or escape the characters properly. For example, "output file.mp4" or output\ file.mp4. Ensure that your FFmpeg version supports the codecs and filters you're using in your FFmpeg command. You can check the documentation or run ffmpeg -codecs and ffmpeg -filters to see the available options. If you encounter issues, consider updating FFmpeg to the latest version. Newer versions often include bug fixes and improved functionality. When an error occurs, carefully review the error message or output provided by FFmpeg. It often provides information about the specific issue encountered. Look for clues such as unsupported codecs, missing dependencies, or incorrect syntax. If you cannot resolve the issue, consider seeking help from the FFmpeg community. There are dedicated forums, mailing lists, and Stack Overflow tags where experienced FFmpeg users can assist you with troubleshooting.

Chapter 4

Graphics Basics-1

C# is a language part of the .NET Framework, which provides a rich set of libraries and tools for developing applications. These libraries include namespaces for working with graphics and Image manipulation, such as the System.Drawing and System.Windows.Media. C# provides access to the Graphics Device Interface Plus (GDI+), a 2D graphics library that allows developers to create and manipulate Images and other graphical elements. GDI+ includes features for drawing shapes, text, and Images and more advanced capabilities like gradient fills, anti-aliasing, and transparency. C# also provides access to the Windows Presentation Foundation (WPF), a robust framework for building desktop applications with advanced graphics and multimedia capabilities. WPF allows developers to create rich, interactive user interfaces that include 2D and 3D graphics, animations, and other visual effects. Many third-party libraries are also available for C#, providing additional graphics and Image manipulation capabilities. These libraries include popular tools like ImageMagick, OpenCV, and SkiaSharp.

I am going through the basics of GDI+ and WPF graphics in this chapter. In the case of GDI+, .Net namespaces System.Drawing, System.Drawing.Drawing2D and System.Drawing.Imaging can be used to create Images, draw graphic objects on Images, and save to formats like JPEG, PNG, GIF, TIFF, BMP, etc. Images can be converted from one format to another and saved to a file.
I can also manipulate Images by resizing, cropping, or applying filters. I can draw basic shapes in WPF and use advanced

graphics required for 2D and 3D animation. WPF has built-in hardware acceleration and resolution independence, making our task easy. Vector graphics in WPF allow us to enlarge any object without getting distorted. WPF also provides a comprehensive set of tools for creating user interfaces, including controls, layout panels, and data binding.

Below I am going through some examples and explaining the drawing of basic shapes in GDI+ and WPF.

Download the source code of all projects/examples covered in this book at https://github.com/Jayasankar-S/CSharp-Animation-And-FFmpeg-Book

Creating and Saving an Image in GDI+

I am starting with creating a simple Image containing a Line on it and saving it to a file in PNG Image format. Below is the code.

```
using System;
using System.Drawing;
using System.Drawing.Imaging;
using System.Drawing.Drawing2D;
using System.Drawing.Text;

Bitmap bmp = new Bitmap(300, 300);
Graphics g = Graphics.FromImage(bmp);

g.SmoothingMode = SmoothingMode.AntiAlias;
g.InterpolationMode = InterpolationMode.HighQualityBicubic;
g.Clear(Color.White);

g.DrawLine(Pens.Black, new Point(100, 150),
        new Point(200, 150));

bmp.Save("SimpleLine.png");
```

First, a Bitmap object is created with a width of 300 pixels and 300 pixels. A graphics object is created from that bitmap.

```
Bitmap bmp = new Bitmap(300, 300);
Graphics g = Graphics.FromImage(bmp);
```

Then the following code is added to improve the quality of the Image.

```
g.SmoothingMode = SmoothingMode.AntiAlias;
g.InterpolationMode = InterpolationMode.HighQualityBicubic;
```

The Image is then filled with a white background using the code,

```
g.Clear(Color.White);
```

In that Image, a black line is drawn from the point (100,150) to (200, 150). I used a black Pen to draw the Line using code,

```
g.DrawLine(Pens.Black, new Point(100, 150),
        new Point(200, 150));
```

I can use an available Pen object from the Pens class or create and use a custom Pen. By default, the thickness of the Line drawn is one pixel. I can change the Pen's thickness by setting the Pen object's Thickness property. In the below code, I am changing the thickness of the Pen object to 10.

```
Pen p = Pens.Black;
p.Thickness = 10;
```

or

```
Pen p = new Pen(Color.Black, 10);
```

Finally, the Image can be saved using the code.

```
bmp.Save("SimpleLine.png");
```

Png is the default Image format, so there is no need to specify the Image format explicitly. On the other hand, for saving as Jpeg format, use the following code.

```
bmp.Save("image.jpg",ImageFormat.Jpeg);
```

Difference Between Pen and Brush

The Pen is used for outlining an object, and the Brush is used for filling an object. For example, the DrawRectangle() method uses a Pen to draw a Rectangle. For the filling, Brush is used in the FillRectangle() method. Different types of Brushes are explained later in this chapter.

Creating and Saving an Image in WPF

In this example, I am creating an Image that contains a Line using WPF. First, I create a Canvas object and add a Line to it as a child, and that Canvas object is later rendered into an Image. Below is the code.

```
using System.Windows;
using System.Windows.Controls;
using System.Windows.Media;
using System.Windows.Media.Imaging;

namespace WpfBasics
{
    public partial class MainWindow: Window
    {
        public MainWindow()
        {
            InitializeComponent();
        }

        private void CreateImage_Click(object sender,
            RoutedEventArgs e)
        {
            Canvas canvas = new Canvas();
            canvas.Measure(new Size(400, 400));
```

```
        canvas.Background = Brushes.White;

        Line line = new Line();
        line.X1 = 100;
        line.Y1 = 100;
        line.X2 = 300;
        line.Y2 = 100;
        line.Stroke = Brushes.Black;
        canvas.Children.Add(line);

        canvas.Arrange(new Rect(new Size(400, 400)));

        RenderTargetBitmap renderTargetBitmap =
            new RenderTargetBitmap(400, 400, 96, 96,
            PixelFormats.Pbgra32);

        renderTargetBitmap.Render(canvas);

        System.IO.FileStream fileStream =
            new System.IO.FileStream("Line.png",
            System.IO.FileMode.Create);

        PngBitmapEncoder pngBitmapEncoder =
            new PngBitmapEncoder();

    pngBitmapEncoder.Frames.Add(
            BitmapFrame.Create(renderTargetBitmap));

        pngBitmapEncoder.Save(fileStream);
        fileStream.Close();

    }
  }
}
```

Here a canvas is created with a width of 400 and height of 400, and the background is set to white. See the below code.

```
Canvas canvas = new Canvas();
canvas.Measure(new Size(400, 400));
```

canvas.Background = Brushes.White;

A Line object is created to draw a Line, and its starting and ending points are set.

```
Line line = new Line();
line.X1 = 100;
line.Y1 = 100;
line.X2 = 300;
line.Y2 = 100;
line.Stroke = Brushes.Black;
canvas.Children.Add(line);
```

The Line.Stroke property specifies the Brushes to be used for outlining the shape. On the other hand, the Line.Fill property is used to specify the Brush used to fill the shape. Here a black Line is drawn from point (100,100) to point (300,100). Line object is added as a child object of Canvas.

```
canvas.Children.Add(line);
```

The Arrange method of the Canvas class will set the Line object in the proper place. To convert, what I have drawn in Canvas to an Image, a RenderTargetBitmap object is created, and Canvas is rendered to that bitmap using code.

```
RenderTargetBitmap renderTargetBitmap =
        new RenderTargetBitmap(400, 400, 96, 96,
        PixelFormats.Pbgra32);

renderTargetBitmap.Render(canvas);
```

It renders the canvas to the RenderTargetBitmap object and saves it as a PNG Image using the code below.

```
System.IO.FileStream fileStream =
        new System.IO.FileStream("Line.png",
        System.IO.FileMode.Create);

PngBitmapEncoder pngBitmapEncoder =
```

```
                    new PngBitmapEncoder();

pngBitmapEncoder.Frames.Add(
              BitmapFrame.Create(renderTargetBitmap));

pngBitmapEncoder.Save(fileStream);
fileStream.Close();
```

Difference Between Stroke and Fill in WPF

Stroke is for outlining a shape, and Fill is for painting the interior of a shape. Unlike in GDI+, in WPF, for Stroke and Fill, Brush is used. For Stroke, I must specify the Stroke Brush; for filling, I must specify the Fill Brush. The StrokeThickness specifies the thickness of the outline drawn.

Drawing a Line with Thickness in WPF

In the following code, the StrokeThickness property of the shape object is used to set the thickness of the outline drawn.

```
Line line = new Line();
line.X1 = 100;
line.Y1 = 100;
line.X2 = 300;
line.Y2 = 100;
line.Stroke = Brushes.Black;
line.StrokeThickness = 5;
canvas.Children.Add(line);
```

Drawing a Rectangle

A Rectangle is drawn starting from the point (50,50) with a width of 200 and a height of 200. Below is the code.

```
Pen pen = new Pen(Color.Black, 10);
```

g.DrawRectangle(pen, 50, 50, 200, 200);

A custom Pen is created with the color black and a thickness of 10.

Pen pen = new Pen(Color.Black, 10);

The DrawRectangle method of the Graphics class is used to outline the Rectangle. The outline drawn will be black and with a thickness of 10.

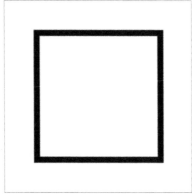

Figure 4-1. Draw Rectangle

Filling a Rectangle with a color

A Rectangle is drawn starting from the point (50,50) with a width of 200 and a height of 200.

g.FillRectangle(Brushes.Black, 50, 50, 200, 200);

Instead of DrawRectangle, the FillRectangle method is used here. The FillRectangle method fills the area specified with the Brush color. Instead of a Pen, a Brush is used here.

Figure 4-2. Fill Rectangle

Drawing a Rectangle in WPF

A Rectangle can be drawn on the Canvas by adding a Rectangle object. The x and y position can be set by static methods SetLeft and SetTop of the Canvas class. The width and height of the Rectangle can be set to the Rectangle object. The following example draws a black Rectangle from position (50,50) to (250,200) without filling it.

```
Rectangle rectangle = new Rectangle();
rectangle.Width = 200;
rectangle.Height = 150;
rectangle.Stroke = Brushes.Black;

Canvas.SetLeft(rectangle, 50);
Canvas.SetTop(rectangle, 50);
canvas.Children.Add(rectangle);
```

Here a Rectangle object is created using code.

```
Rectangle rectangle = new Rectangle();
```

After that, its width and height are set. The Stroke parameter value is set with the black Brush, and the Fill Brush parameter value is not set. So, Rectangle is drawn without filling inside, and only an outline is drawn.

```
rectangle.Width = 200;
rectangle.Height = 150;
rectangle.Stroke = Brushes.Black;
```

The x and y position can be set by static methods SetLeft and SetTop of the Canvas class.

```
Canvas.SetLeft(rectangle, 50);
Canvas.SetTop(rectangle, 50);
```

Figure 4-3. WPF-Draw Rectangle

Filling the Rectangle in WPF

I need to use a Brush to set the Fill property of the Rectangle class to fill a Rectangle. The below code demonstrates how to fill a Rectangle with gray color.

```
Rectangle rectangle = new Rectangle();
rectangle.Width = 200;
rectangle.Height = 150;
rectangle.Fill = Brushes.Gray;

Canvas.SetLeft(rectangle, 50);
Canvas.SetTop(rectangle, 50);
```

canvas.Children.Add(rectangle);

Here in this example, the code

rectangle.Fill = Brushes.Gray;

is setting the Fill property. I can use a custom Brush instead of the ready-made Brushes available in the Brushes class. More about custom Brushes are explained in the next chapter.

Figure 4-4. WPF-Fill Rectangle

Rounded Rectangle in WPF

In the above section, I draw Rectangles with sharp corners. I can draw Rectangles with rounded corners in WPF using the RadiusX and RadiusY properties of the Rectangle class. The below code demonstrates drawing a rounded corner Rectangle.

```
Rectangle rectangle = new Rectangle();
rectangle.Width = 200;
rectangle.Height = 150;
rectangle.RadiusX = 50;
rectangle.RadiusY = 50;
rectangle.Stroke = Brushes.Black;
```

```
Canvas.SetLeft(rectangle, 50);
Canvas.SetTop(rectangle, 50);
canvas.Children.Add(rectangle);
```

The code

```
rectangle.RadiusX = 50;
rectangle.RadiusY = 50;
```

Changes the radius of the corners of the Rectangle.

Figure 4-5. WPF-Rectangle with rounded corners

Drawing a Transparent Rectangle
In this example, I am filling two Rectangles with transparent colors. Below is the code.

```
Color transparentGray = Color.FromArgb(125,Color.Gray);
Brush transparentGrayBrush = new SolidBrush(transparentGray);
g.FillRectangle(transparentGrayBrush, 50, 50, 150, 150);
g.FillRectangle(transparentGrayBrush, 100, 100, 150, 150);
bmp.Save("TransparentRectangle.png");
```

I draw two transparent gray color Rectangles which are overlapping each other. To draw a transparent shape, I need a Brush with transparent color. To create a transparent color, the following code is used.

Color transparentGray = Color.FromArgb(125,Color.Gray);

Here Color.FromArgb method takes an alpha value ranging from 0 to 255. 0 means completely transparent, and 255 means completely opaque. In our case, I am using the value 125, which means semitransparent. The next value I passed was a gray color. So, the Color.FromArgb method returns a transparent version of the color I have given. I can create a transparent color directly by giving alpha, red, green, and blue values to the same method as the code below.

Color transparentGray = Color.FromArgb(125,128, 128, 128);

Figure 4-6. Transparent Rectangle

Drawing a Transparent Rectangle in WPF

Like GDI+, I need a Brush with transparent color to draw a transparent shape in WPF. The following example demonstrates how to draw two Rectangles overlapping each other using transparent gray color.

```
SolidColorBrush solidColorBrush =
new SolidColorBrush(Color.FromArgb(125, 100, 100, 100));

Rectangle rectangle = new Rectangle();
rectangle.Width = 150;
rectangle.Height = 150;
rectangle.Fill = solidColorBrush;

Canvas.SetLeft(rectangle,50);
Canvas.SetTop(rectangle, 50);
canvas.Children.Add(rectangle);

Rectangle rectangle2 = new Rectangle();
rectangle2.Width = 150;
rectangle2.Height = 150;
rectangle2.Fill = solidColorBrush;

Canvas.SetLeft(rectangle2, 100);
Canvas.SetTop(rectangle2, 100);
canvas.Children.Add(rectangle2);
```

The code

```
Color.FromArgb(125, 100, 100, 100)
```

Creates a transparent color, and that transparent color is used to create a transparent Brush.

```
SolidColorBrush solidColorBrush =
new SolidColorBrush(Color.FromArgb(125, 100, 100, 100));
```

Here the alpha value used is 125. So, the Rectangles are filled with semitransparent gray color.

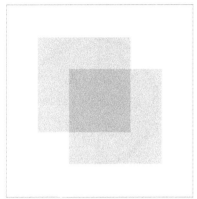

Figure 4-7. WPF-Transparent Rectangles

Drawing a Circle

A Circle can be drawn using the DrawEllipse method of Graphics class. The DrawEllipse method takes a Pen object and a Rectangle object or Rectangle values such as Rectangle start positions x, y, width, and height. If I pass a Square(width and height are the same), then a Circle is drawn, and if I pass a Rectangle (width and height different), an Ellipse is drawn. Similarly, like the DrawEllipse method, the FillEllipse method fills the Circle using a Brush.

```
Pen pen = new Pen(Color.Black, 10);
g.DrawEllipse(pen, 50, 50, 200, 200);
bmp.Save("Circle.png");
```

The code

```
g.DrawEllipse(pen, 50, 50, 200, 200);
```

draws a Circle with a radius 100, which is half the Rectangle's width/height. Starting point of a Circle is point (50, 50). So the center will be at point (150,150).

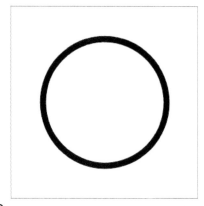

Figure 4-8. Circle

Drawing an Ellipse

The following code draws an Ellipse instead of a Circle.

```
Pen pen = new Pen(Color.Black, 10);
g.DrawEllipse(pen, new RectangleF(50, 100, 200, 100));
bmp.Save("Ellipse.png");
```

If the width and height of the Rectangle object are different, then the DrawEllipse method draws an Ellipse. Here DrawEllipse method will draw an Ellipse with 200 pixels x diameter and 100 pixels y diameter.

```
g.DrawEllipse(pen, new RectangleF(50, 50, 200, 100));
```

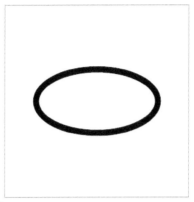

Figure 4-9. Ellipse

Drawing a Circle in WPF

The Circle can be drawn using the Ellipse class in WPF. x and y positions can be set by static functions SetLeft and SetTop of the Canvas class. The width and height of the Circle can be set to the Ellipse object.

```
Ellipse ellipse = new Ellipse();
ellipse.Width = 200;
ellipse.Height = 200;
ellipse.StrokeThickness = 5;
ellipse.Stroke = Brushes.Black;

Canvas.SetLeft(ellipse, 50);
Canvas.SetTop(ellipse, 50);

canvas.Children.Add(ellipse);
```

The Code

```
Ellipse ellipse = new Ellipse();
ellipse.Width = 200;
ellipse.Height = 200;
```

Creates an Ellipse object and sets its width and height. A Circle is drawn with a radius of 100, which is half of the width/height, and with a center point (150,150).

If the width and height of the Ellipse object are different, then the resultant shape will be an Ellipse instead of a Circle.

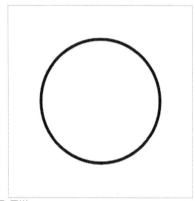

Figure 4-10. WPF-Ellipse

Drawing an Arc

Drawing an Arc is the same as drawing an Ellipse or Circle, but the only additional thing required is the start and sweep angles. An Arc is a portion of an Ellipse. So, I have to specify which portion I have to draw. 360 degrees make a full Circle or Ellipse. So, the start angle is the angle at which the Arc starts. Sweep angle means the Arc ends after that many degrees from the start angle. In the example below, I am drawing an Arc with 70 degrees starting from 280 degrees.

```
Pen pen = new Pen(Color.Black, 10);
RectangleF rect = new RectangleF(50, 50, 200, 200);
g.DrawArc(pen, rect, 280,70);
bmp.Save("Arc.png");
```

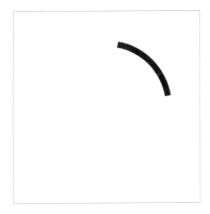

Figure 4-11. Arc

The following figure shows the same Arc with coordinates.

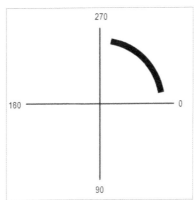

Figure 4-12. Arc with coordinates

Drawing an Arc in WPF

Drawing an Arc in WPF is more complicated than drawing the other shapes discussed earlier. I use Path, PathFigure, and ArcSegment classes to draw an Arc.

ArcSegment takes the following parameters.

• Point: The starting point of the Arc.

- Size: The horizontal and vertical radius of the Arc.

  - rotationAngle: Rotation angle of the segment. Zero value means no rotation. Otherwise, the Arc is rotated in degrees by that much value.

  - isLargeArc: A total of four Arcs can be drawn between two points. Two Large Arcs can be drawn opposite each other(like one Arc is a mirror Image of another if a straight line between points is considered the mirror). Similarly, two small Arcs can also be drawn from one point to another, opposite each other. A large Arc is an Arc greater than 180 degrees. By default, the Arc is drawn in a clockwise direction.

  - sweepDirection: Direction of drawing. Clockwise or anti-clockwise.

- isStroked: Set to true to stroke the Arc.

To draw an Arc, an ArcSegment object is added to the segments collection of PathFigure. PathFigure object is then added to the Path object. This Path object is added to the canvas as a shape. The following code adds an Arc between points (50,50) and (50,250) in a clockwise direction, with a radius of 50.

```
Point point = new Point(50, 250);
Size size = new Size(100, 100);
ArcSegment arc =
                new ArcSegment(point, size, 0, true,
SweepDirection.Clockwise, true);

PathFigure pathFigure = new PathFigure();
pathFigure.StartPoint = new Point(50, 50);
pathFigure.Segments.Add(arc);
pathFigure.IsClosed = false;
Path path = new Path();

path.Stroke = Brushes.Black;
path.StrokeThickness = 2;
```

```
path.Data = new PathGeometry(new PathFigure[] { pathFigure });
```

```
Canvas.SetLeft(path, 0);
Canvas.SetTop(path, 0);
canvas.Children.Add(path);
```

The code

```
Point point = new Point(50, 250);
Size size = new Size(100, 100);
ArcSegment arc =  new ArcSegment(point, size, 0, true,
            SweepDirection.Clockwise, true);
```

Creates an ArcSegment with starting point (50,50) and an ending point (50,250). Size is (100, 100), so the Arc is of radius 100 points. The rotation angle is zero and is a large Arc with SweepDirection clockwise.

The following code creates a Pathfigure object and adds an ArcSegment object.

```
PathFigure pathFigure = new PathFigure();
pathFigure.StartPoint = new Point(50, 50);
pathFigure.Segments.Add(arc);
pathFigure.IsClosed = false;
```

This PathFigure object is added to the PathGeometry object. PathGeometry class represents a complex shape. Then PathGeometry object is set as the value of the Data property of the Path object.

```
Path path = new Path();
path.Stroke = Brushes.Black;
path.StrokeThickness = 2;
path.Data = new PathGeometry(new PathFigure[] { pathFigure });
```

Finally, the Path object is added to Canvas, and the Canvas object is rendered to an Image.

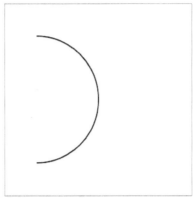

Figure 4-13. WPF-Arc

Drawing an Image

First, I must load an Image from a file or create an Image object to draw an Image. In this case, I am loading an existing Image file.

```
Image image = Image.FromFile("flower.jpg");
g.DrawImage(image, 50, 50, 200, 200);
bmp.Save("OutputImage.png");
```

The DrawImage method draws the Image to the Rectangle given.

```
g.DrawImage(image, 50, 50, 200, 200);
```

Here a Rectangle starts from point(50,50) with a width of 200 and height of 200. If the source Image is bigger or smaller than the Rectangle, it is scaled to the dimensions of the target Rectangle.

Figure 4-14. Drawn Image

Drawing an Image in WPF

To draw an Image in WPF Canvas, I need to create an Image object and should set the source property of that Image object with the BitmapImage object. Here the BitmapImage object is created by loading an Image from a file. After that, the Image object can be added to the canvas as a child.

```
Image image = new Image();

image.Source = new BitmapImage(
        new Uri(@"flower.jpg", UriKind.RelativeOrAbsolute));

image.HorizontalAlignment = HorizontalAlignment.Left;
image.Width = 200;
image.Height = 200;

Canvas.SetLeft(image,50);
Canvas.SetTop(image, 50);
canvas.Children.Add(image);
```

A BitmapImage object is created, which loads an Image from an Image file and is added as a source of an Image object.

```
Image image = new Image();
image.Source = new BitmapImage(
```

new Uri(@"flower.jpg", UriKind.RelativeOrAbsolute));

Rendering width and height can be set to the Image object. After that, this Image object is added to the Canvas object as a child.

```
image.HorizontalAlignment = HorizontalAlignment.Left;
image.Width = 200;
image.Height = 200;
```

Figure 4-15. WPF-Drawn Image

Drawing a Pie

Drawing a Pie is the same as drawing an Arc. A Pie is part of a Circle or an Ellipse enclosed by radii on both sides. To draw a Pie, I have to pass a Rectangle object, a start angle, and a sweep angle.

```
Pen pen = new Pen(Color.Black, 10);
g.DrawPie(pen, new RectangleF(50, 50, 200, 200),225,90);
bmp.Save("Pie.png");
```

The code

```
g.DrawPie(pen, new RectangleF(50, 50, 200, 200),225,90);
```

draws a Pie from an angle of 225 degrees to 225+ 90 degrees. Here 225 degrees is the start angle, and 90 degrees is the sweep angle.

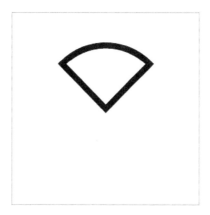

Figure 4-16. Pie

Drawing a Pie in WPF

Drawing a Pie in WPF is more complex than in GDI+. WPF does not have a DrawPie method like GDI+. So, to draw a Pie, I need to use PathFigure, PathGeometry, and Path classes. PathFigure contains connected segments to define a figure. PathGeometry, which represents a complex shape,   contains a collection of PathFigures. PathFigures array is set as the Data property value of the Path object, and this Path object will be added to the Canvas class as a child.

```
int radius = 150;
Point centrePoint = new Point(100,250);

Point arcStartPoint = new Point(
            centrePoint.X, centrePoint.Y – radius);

Point arcEndPoint = new Point(
            centrePoint.X + radius, centrePoint.Y);

PathFigure pathFigure = new PathFigure();
```

```
pathFigure.StartPoint = arcStartPoint;

ArcSegment arc =
        new ArcSegment(arcEndPoint, new Size(radius, radius),
        0, false, SweepDirection.Clockwise, true);
        path figure.Segments.Add(arc);

LineSegment line1 = new LineSegment(centrePoint, true);

pathFigure.Segments.Add(line1);

LineSegment line2 = new LineSegment(arcStartPoint, true);
pathFigure.Segments.Add(line2);

Path path = new Path();

path.Stroke = Brushes.Black;
path.Fill = Brushes.LightGray;
path.Data = new PathGeometry(new PathFigure[] { pathFigure });

Canvas.SetLeft(path, 0);
Canvas.SetTop(path, 0);

canvas.Children.Add(path);
```

To create a Pie, three segments (two LineSegments and one ArcSegment) are added to the PathFigure object. ArcSegment represents the curved part of the Pie, and two line segments represent both sides of the Pie. When added to PathFigure, these segments merge to become a Pie shape. The following code creates three points. The first is the Centrepoint, which defines the center of the Arc; the second is the arcStartPoint which is the point at which the Arc starts. And third one is the arcEndPoint which is the Arc ending point.

```
int radius = 150;
Point centrePoint = new Point(100,250);

Point arcStartPoint =
        new Point(centrePoint.X, centrePoint.Y - radius);
```

```
Point arcEndPoint =
        new Point(centrePoint.X + radius, centrePoint.Y);
```

Next, a PathFigure object is created, setting the StartPoint as the Arc start point.

```
PathFigure pathFigure = new PathFigure();
pathFigure.StartPoint = arcStartPoint;
```

Next, three segments are added to the PathFigure object, two LineSegments, and one ArcSegment. So, these three segments together create a Pie shape.

```
ArcSegment arc =
        new ArcSegment(arcEndPoint, new Size(radius, radius),
        0, false, SweepDirection.Clockwise, true);
        path figure.Segments.Add(arc);
```

```
LineSegment line1 = new LineSegment(centrePoint, true);
pathFigure.Segments.Add(line1);
```

```
LineSegment line2 = new LineSegment(arcStartPoint, true);
pathFigure.Segments.Add(line2);
```

After that pathFigure is added to the Path object, and that Path object is added to Canvas as a child.

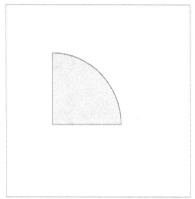

Figure 4-17. WPF-Pie

Drawing a Pentagon

Here I am creating a custom shape using the DrawPolygon method. A Pentagon has five sides, and I am drawing a Pentagon using five Lines. The DrawPolygon method takes a Pen object and an array of points. Lines are drawn between points; at the end, the start and end points are joined by a Line to complete the polygon.

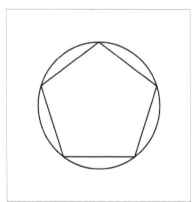

Figure 4-18. Finding the Pentagon points

Following is the full code to draw a Pentagon.

```
Pen p = new Pen(Color.Black, 2);

Point origin = new Point(150,150);
double radius = 100;

List<PointF> starPoints = new List<PointF>();
for (int angle = -18; angle < 342; angle = angle + 72)
{
    double x = Math.Cos(angle * Math.PI / 180) * radius;
    double y = Math.Sin(angle * Math.PI / 180) * radius;

    starPoints.Add(
        new PointF((float)x + origin.X, (float)y + origin.Y));
}

g.DrawPolygon(p, starPoints.ToArray());
bmp.Save("pentagon.png");
```

I am using the Circle equation to get the points required to draw the Pentagon. The total degree of a Circle is 360. If I divide it by five, I will get 72 degrees. So the trick is to take points from the circumference of the Circle with 72 degrees angular distance. Then I will get five points. These points are the vertices of the Pentagon.

The code

```
Point origin = new Point(150,150);
double radius = 100;

List<PointF> starPoints = new List<PointF>();
for (int angle = -18; angle < 342; angle = angle + 72)
{
    double x = Math.Cos(angle * Math.PI / 180) * radius;
    double y = Math.Sin(angle * Math.PI / 180) * radius;

    starPoints.Add(
        new PointF((float)x + origin.X, (float)y + origin.Y));
}
```

gets the points of a Pentagon around the origin point. Pentagon is starting at -18 degrees and ending at 342 degrees (-18 + 360 = 342). The angle variable is multiplied by (Math.PI / 180). This is to convert from degree to radian.

Drawing a Pentagon using GraphicsPath

Here I am explaining another way of drawing a Pentagon. Graphicspath is used here instead of the DrawPolygon method. The same Circle logic is used to get the Pentagon vertices. After getting the points, Lines are added using Graphicspath.AddLine method. Graphicspath creates a closed figure using these Lines and draws to the Image.

```
Pen p = new Pen(Color.Black, 10);

Point origin = new Point(150, 150);
double radius = 100;

List<PointF> starPoints = new List<PointF>();
for (int angle = -18; angle < 342; angle = angle + 72)
{
        double x = Math.Cos(angle * Math.PI / 180) * radius;
        double y = Math.Sin(angle * Math.PI / 180) * radius;
        starPoints.Add(
          new PointF((float)x + origin.X, (float)y + origin.Y));
}

PointF p1 = starPoints[0];
PointF p2 = starPoints[1];
PointF p3 = starPoints[2];
PointF p4 = starPoints[3];
PointF p5 = starPoints[4];

GraphicsPath path = new GraphicsPath();

path.StartFigure();
```

```
path.AddLine(p1, p2);
path.AddLine(p2, p3);
path.AddLine(p3, p4);
path.AddLine(p4, p5);
path.AddLine(p5, p1);
path.CloseFigure();

g.DrawPath(p, path);
bmp.Save("pentagonWithGrapicsPath.png");
```

The code

```
GraphicsPath path = new GraphicsPath();
path.StartFigure();
path.AddLine(p1, p2);
path.AddLine(p2, p3);
path.AddLine(p3, p4);
path.AddLine(p4, p5);
path.AddLine(p5, p1);
path.CloseFigure();

g.DrawPath(p, path);
```

adds five Lines, which are the sides of the Pentagon. Graphics DrawPath method uses these Lines to create a polygon and draws to the Image.

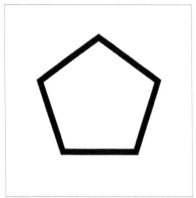

Figure 4-19. Pentagon

Drawing a Pentagon in WPF

Like the Pie shape drawn in an earlier example, the same PathFigure class is used here to draw a Pentagon. A Pentagon has five sides. So five LineSegments are created and added to the PathFigure to create a Pentagon. Below is the code.

```
double y = 0;
double radius = 100;

double xStart = Math.Cos(0 * Math.PI / 180) * radius;

List<Point> starPoints = new List<Point>();
for (int angle = 0; angle < 360; angle = angle + 72)
{
        double x = Math.Cos(angle * Math.PI / 180) * radius;
        y = Math.Sin(angle * Math.PI / 180) * radius;
        starPoints.Add(new Point(x + 100, y + 100));
}

  Point p1 = starPoints[0];
  Point p2 = starPoints[1];
  Point p3 = starPoints[2];
  Point p4 = starPoints[3];
  Point p5 = starPoints[4];
```

```
PathFigure pathFigure = new PathFigure();
pathFigure.StartPoint = p1;

LineSegment line1 = new LineSegment(p2, true);
pathFigure.Segments.Add(line1);

LineSegment line2 = new LineSegment(p3, true);
pathFigure.Segments.Add(line2);

LineSegment line3 = new LineSegment(p4, true);
pathFigure.Segments.Add(line3);

LineSegment line4 = new LineSegment(p5, true);
pathFigure.Segments.Add(line4);

LineSegment line5 = new LineSegment(p1, true);
pathFigure.Segments.Add(line5);

Path path = new Path();

path.Stroke = Brushes.Black;
path.Fill = Brushes.LightGray;
path.Data = new PathGeometry(new PathFigure[] { pathFigure });

Canvas.SetLeft(path, 100);
Canvas.SetTop(path, 100);

canvas.Children.Add(path);
```

When five LineSegments are added to PathFigure, these segments merge to become a Pentagon shape.

Figure 4-20. WPF - Pentagon

Drawing a Text

The Graphics.DrawString method is used to draw text. The DrawString method takes the text to be drawn as the first parameter and the font object as the second parameter. A font object can be created using the code.

Font font = new Font("Arial", 16);

The third parameter is Brush type. Here black Brush is specified. The fourth parameter is the point at which the text should be drawn.

Font font = new Font("Arial", 30);

g.DrawString(
        "Sample Text", font, Brushes.Black, new PointF(25, 25));
bmp.Save("Text.png");

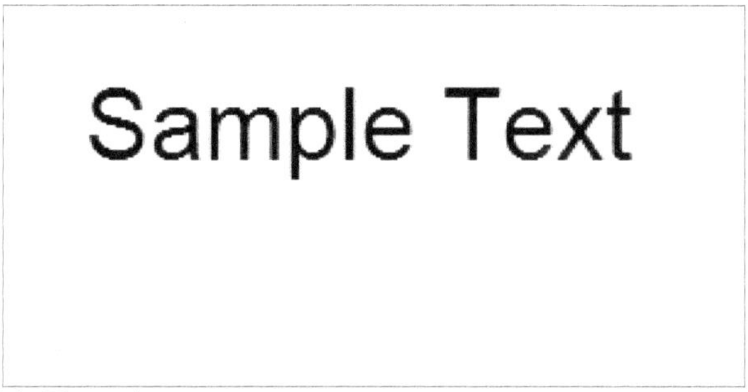

Sample Text

Figure 4-21. Text drawn

Drawing a Text in WPF

To draw a text in Canvas, a TextBlock object is created, its Text, FontSize, and Foreground properties are set, and that TextBlock object is added to the Canvas.

```
TextBlock textBlock = new TextBlock();
textBlock.Text = "Sample text";
textBlock.FontSize = 60;
textBlock.Foreground = new SolidColorBrush(Colors.Gray);
Canvas.SetLeft(textBlock, 50);
Canvas.SetTop(textBlock, 50);
canvas.Children.Add(textBlock);
```

Figure 4-22. WPF-Text drawn

Chapter 5

Graphics Basics-2

In the last chapter, I explained drawing basic shapes in WPF and GDI+. In this chapter, I am explaining more about path-based shapes. Path-based logic allows you to create complicated shapes using basic shapes like Lines, Rectangles, Ellipses, arcs, Bezier curves, etc.

In WPF, classes inherited from PathSegment, like ArcSegment, BezierSegment, LineSegment, PolyBezierSegment, PolyLineSegment, QuadraticBezierSegment, and PolyQuadraticBezierSegment can be used to build a PathFigure. Each segment type has its purpose usage. Some of these segments I am using in the below-given examples.

In the case of GDI+, GraphicsPath class is used for similar purposes. To build a complex figure, I can create a GraphicsPath object and add basic shapes like Rectangles, Ellipses, Lines, arcs, text, etc. GraphicsPath is simple to use, and I can access the point array of the figure and manually change it if required.

Download the source code of all projects/examples covered in this book at https://github.com/Jayasankar-S/CSharp-Animation-And-FFmpeg-Book

Drawing a Star

The DrawPolygon method of the Graphics class takes two parameters, a Pen object and an array of points. The

DrawPolygon method draws a polygon using points starting from the first point to the last point.

I am using the Circle equation in the Pentagon example to get the points required to draw the star. I am taking five points from the circumference of the Circle, with 72 degrees angular distance. These five points are used to draw the star shape. Below is the code.

```
Pen p = new Pen(Color.Black, 10);

double y = 0;
double radius = 100;

Point origin = new Point(150, 150);

List<PointF> starPoints = new List<PointF>();
for (int angle = -55; angle < 305; angle = angle + 72)
{
    double x = Math.Cos(angle * Math.PI / 180) * radius;
    y = Math.Sin(angle * Math.PI / 180) * radius;

    starPoints.Add(
        new PointF((float)x + origin.X, (float)y + origin.Y));
}

PointF p1 = starPoints[0];
PointF p2 = starPoints[1];
PointF p3 = starPoints[2];
PointF p4 = starPoints[3];
PointF p5 = starPoints[4];

g.DrawPolygon(p, new PointF[] { p1, p4, p2, p5, p3, p1 });
bmp.Save("star.png");
```

Figure 5-1. Points of Star

Drawing a Star using GraphicsPath

The same star can be drawn using the DrawPath method. As in the above case, five points in the Circle with an angular distance of 72 degrees were generated using the Circle equation. Five Lines of the star were added to the GraphicsPath object using that points.

```
Pen p = new Pen(Color.Black, 10);

double y = 0;
double radius = 100;
Point origin = new Point(150, 150);

List<PointF> starPoints = new List<PointF>();
for (int angle = -55; angle < 305; angle = angle + 72)
{
    double x = Math.Cos(angle * Math.PI / 180) * radius;
    y = Math.Sin(angle * Math.PI / 180) * radius;
    starPoints.Add(
        new PointF((float)x + origin.X, (float)y + origin.Y));
}

PointF p1 = starPoints[0];
PointF p2 = starPoints[1];
PointF p3 = starPoints[2];
PointF p4 = starPoints[3];
PointF p5 = starPoints[4];
```

```
GraphicsPath path = new GraphicsPath();

path.AddLine(p1, p4);
path.AddLine(p4, p2);
path.AddLine(p2, p5);
path.AddLine(p5, p3);
path.AddLine(p3, p1);

path.CloseFigure();

g.DrawPath(p, path);
bmp.Save("star2.png");
```

The output of the code is the same as in the previous example.

Drawing a Star in WPF

I am using LineSegment and PathFigure classes to draw a star in WPF. Five points are created using the Circle equation, as in the GraphicsPath example. Below is the code.

```
Canvas canvas = new Canvas();
canvas.Measure(new Size(400, 400));
canvas.Background = Brushes.White;

double y = 0;
double radius = 100;

double xStart = Math.Cos(0 * Math.PI / 180) * radius;

List<Point> starPoints = new List<Point>();
for (int angle = 0; angle < 360; angle = angle + 72)
{
    double x = Math.Cos(angle * Math.PI / 180) * radius;
    y = Math.Sin(angle * Math.PI / 180) * radius;
    starPoints.Add(new Point(x + 100, y + 100));
}

Point p1 = starPoints[0];
Point p2 = starPoints[1];
```

```
Point p3 = starPoints[2];
Point p4 = starPoints[3];
Point p5 = starPoints[4];

PathFigure pathFigure = new PathFigure();
pathFigure.StartPoint = p1;

LineSegment line1 = new LineSegment(p4, true);
pathFigure.Segments.Add(line1);

LineSegment line2 = new LineSegment(p2, true);
pathFigure.Segments.Add(line2);

LineSegment line3 = new LineSegment(p5, true);
pathFigure.Segments.Add(line3);

LineSegment line4 = new LineSegment(p3, true);
pathFigure.Segments.Add(line4);

LineSegment line5 = new LineSegment(p1, true);
pathFigure.Segments.Add(line5);

Path path = new Path();

path.Stroke = Brushes.Black;

path.Data = new PathGeometry(new PathFigure[] { pathFigure });

Canvas.SetLeft(path, 100);
Canvas.SetTop(path, 100);

canvas.Children.Add(path);
canvas.Arrange(new Rect(new Size(400, 400)));
```

The Line segments are created from points and added to the PathFigure object. Here line1 is drawn from pathFigure.StartPoint, which is p1 to p4. The next Line is drawn from p4 to p2; that way, five LineSegments are added to create the complete star shape.

Figure 5-2. WPF-Star

Drawing Text With Outline

Drawing a text to an Image can be done using the DrawString method of the Graphics class. I can draw using any font or color. Adding an outline to the text is impossible using the DrawString method. For that, I have to use the GraphicsPath class. When I add a string to the graphics path, each glyph in the input text is converted to points and curves and stored as an array in the GraphicsPath object. Once converted text to a GraphicsPath object, we can draw an outline using a Pen and can fill the text shape with a brush. Below is the code.

```
Pen pen = new Pen(Color.Black, 10);
pen.LineJoin = LineJoin.Round;

GraphicsPath graphicsPath = new GraphicsPath();

graphicsPath.AddString("Sample Text",
        FontFamily.GenericSansSerif, (int)FontStyle.Regular,
        40, new Point(50, 50), new StringFormat());

g.FillPath(Brushes.Gray, graphicsPath);
g.DrawPath(Pens.Black, graphicsPath);

bmp.Save("TextOutline1.png");
```

Figure 5-3. Text outline

Drawing Text With Outline in WPF

I am using the Typeface, FormattedText, and Geometry classes to draw a text with an outline in WPF. Below is the code.

```
Canvas canvas = new Canvas();
Size canvasSize = new Size(400, 400);
canvas.Measure(canvasSize);
canvas.Background = Brushes.White;


System.Windows.FontStyle fontStyle =
        FontStyles.Normal;

FontWeight fontWeight = FontWeights.Medium;

Typeface typeface =
        new Typeface(new FontFamily("Comic Sans MS"),
        fontStyle, fontWeight, FontStretches.Normal);

FormattedText formattedText =
    new FormattedText("Text", CultureInfo.GetCultureInfo("en-us"),
    FlowDirection.LeftToRight, typeface, 100,
    System.Windows.Media.Brushes.Black, 96);

Geometry textGeometry =
```

```
formattedText.BuildGeometry(
    new System.Windows.Point(0, 0));

Path path = new Path();

path.Stroke = Brushes.Black;
path.Fill = Brushes.Gray;
path.StrokeThickness = 5;
path.Data = textGeometry;

Canvas.SetLeft(path, 100);
Canvas.SetTop(path, 100);

canvas.Children.Add(path);
canvas.Arrange(new Rect(canvasSize));
```

The BuildGeometry method of the FormattedText class creates a Geometry object, and this Geometry object can be set as the value of the Data property of the Path class object. Once the Path object is created, I can set the FillBrush, StrokeBrush, and StrokeThickness values. As a result, the Text is Drawn on the canvas using the FillBrush, and the outline is drawn using the StrokeBrush.

Drawing text in the center of the Image

To draw text in the center of a Rectangle or an Image, the size of that text is to be measured first. This can be accomplished using the MeasureString method of the Graphics class. Below is the code.

```
int textEmSize = 70;
Font font= new
System.Drawing.Font(FontFamily.GenericSansSerif, textEmSize,
        (int)FontStyle.Regular, GraphicsUnit.Pixel);

SizeF size = g.MeasureString("Text", font);
```

```
int textX = (bmp.Width - (int)size. Width) / 2;
int textY = (bmp.Height - (int)size.Height) / 2;

GraphicsPath path = new GraphicsPath();

path.AddString("Text", FontFamily.GenericSansSerif,
        (int)FontStyle.Regular, textEmSize,
        new Point(textX, textY), new StringFormat());

g.FillPath(Brushes.LightGray,path);

Pen p = new Pen(Color.Black, 3);
p.LineJoin = LineJoin.Round;
g.DrawPath(p,path);

bmp.Save("text.png");
```

The Line

```
SizeF size = g.MeasureString("Text", font);
```

measures the size of the text. Then point at which the text is to be drawn is calculated using the code.

```
int textX = (bmp.Width - (int)size. Width) / 2;
int textY = (bmp.Height - (int)size.Height) / 2;
```

Figure 5-4. With textEmSize = 70

Figure 5-5. With textEmSize = 100

Figure 5-6. With textEmSize = 150

Drawing text in the center of the Image In WPF

To draw the text in the center of the canvas, as in the earlier example, I have to measure the size of the text, and based on that size, I have to calculate the place where I have to place the text. Below is the code.

```
Canvas canvas = new Canvas();
Size canvasSize = new Size(400, 400);
canvas.Measure(canvasSize);
canvas.Background = Brushes.White;


System.Windows.FontStyle fontStyle = FontStyles.Normal;
FontWeight fontWeight = FontWeights.Medium;

Typeface typeface =
    new Typeface(new FontFamily("Comic Sans MS"),
    fontStyle, fontWeight, FontStretches.Normal);

FormattedText formattedText =
    new FormattedText("Text", CultureInfo.GetCultureInfo("en-us"),
```

```
FlowDirection.LeftToRight, typeface, 100,
System.Windows.Media.Brushes.Black, 90);

Geometry textGeometry = formattedText.BuildGeometry(
    new System.Windows.Point(
    (canvasSize.Width - formattedText.Width) / 2,
    (canvasSize.Height - formattedText.Height) / 2));

Path path = new Path();

path.Stroke = Brushes.Black;
path.Fill = Brushes.Gray;
path.StrokeThickness = 5;
path.Data = textGeometry;

canvas.Children.Add(path);
canvas.Arrange(new Rect(canvasSize));
```

The code

```
Geometry textGeometry = formattedText.BuildGeometry(
    new System.Windows.Point((canvasSize.Width -
    formattedText.Width)/2, (canvasSize.Height -
    formattedText.Height) / 2));
```

places the text in the vertical and horizontal middle of the canvas. When the text size increases, the text position is adjusted accordingly.

Drawing a Balloon

In this example, I am drawing a balloon shape using GraphicsPath. The AddBezier method takes four points as parameters, where the first and last points are the start and endpoints. The second and third points are control points that bend the Line. The CloseFigure() method will draw a line between the start and end points if they are different. In this example, I am using only one Bezier curve. The shape I create will be more realistic if I create it using more curves. Below is the code.

```
Point point = new Point(150, 150);

GraphicsPath graphicsPath = new GraphicsPath();
graphics path.StartFigure();

graphics path.AddBezier(
    new Point(147,152), new Point(290, 30), new Point(10, 30),
    new Point(152, 152));

graphics path.CloseFigure();

Pen pen = new Pen(Color.Black, 5);
g.DrawPath(pen, graphicsPath);

bmp.Save("Balloon.png");
```

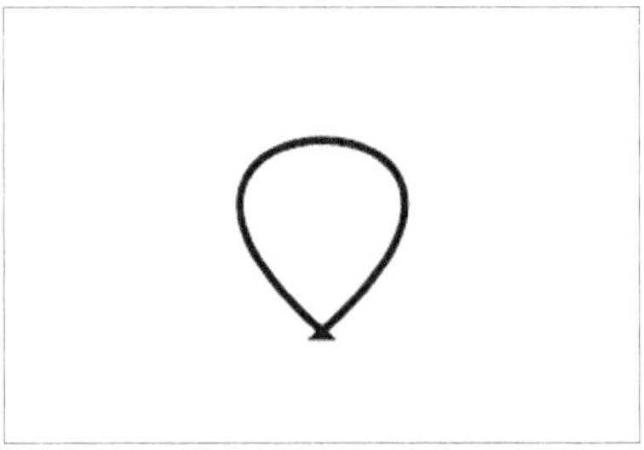

Figure 5-7. Balloon

Drawing a Balloon in WPF

To draw a balloon in WPF, PolyQuadraticBezierSegment class is used. A PolyQuadraticBezierSegment object was created, and five controlling points were used to get the balloon shape. Below is the code.

```
Canvas canvas = new Canvas();
Size canvasSize = new Size(400, 400);
canvas.Measure(canvasSize);
canvas.Background = Brushes.White;

Point point1 = new Point(190, 280);
Point point2 = new Point(350, 70);
```

```
Point point3 = new Point(200, 60);
Point point4 = new Point(50, 70);
Point point5 = new Point(210, 280);

PointCollection pointCollection =
    new PointCollection { point2, point3, point4, point5 };

PolyQuadraticBezierSegment polyQuadraticBezierSegment =
    new PolyQuadraticBezierSegment(pointCollection, true);

PathFigure pathFigure = new PathFigure();
pathFigure.StartPoint = point1;
pathFigure.Segments.Add(polyQuadraticBezierSegment);
pathFigure.IsClosed = false;
Path path = new Path();

path.Stroke = Brushes.Black;
path.StrokeThickness = 5;

path.Data = new PathGeometry(new PathFigure[] { pathFigure });

canvas.Children.Add(path);
canvas.Arrange(new Rect(canvasSize));
```

Figure 5-8. WPF-Balloon

Different Types of Brushes

Pen is used to outline the shape. Brushes are used to fill the interior of a closed shape. There are four types of brushes in GDI+, which I explained below with examples.

Solid Brush

A SolidBrush is used to fill a shape with solid colors. SolidBrush represents a single solid color. The SolidBrush constructor takes a color as the parameter.

SolidBrush solidBush = new SolidBrush(Color.LightGray);
g.FillRectangle(solidBush, new Rectangle(50,50,100,100));
bmp.Save("solidBush.png");

Figure 5-9. SolidBrush

Hatch Brush

HatchBrush is used to fill with a line pattern in different directions. The HatchBrush constructor takes three parameters, HatchStyle, foreground color, and background color. Pattern HatchBrush draws based on HatchStyle. Below I am showing different kinds of patterns created with HatchBrush.

HatchBrush hatchBrush = new HatchBrush(HatchStyle.Cross,
        Color.Black, Color.LightGray);

g.FillRectangle(hatchBrush, new Rectangle(50, 50, 100, 100));
bmp.Save("hatchBrush.png");

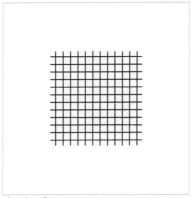

Figure 5-10. HatchStyle.Cross

Figure 5-11. HatchStyle.Sphere

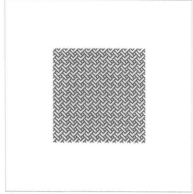

Figure 5-12. HatchStyle.Weave

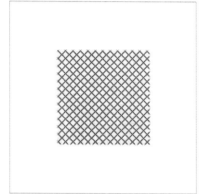

Figure 5-13. HatchStyle.OutlinedDiamond

Texture Brush

If I want to fill with a pattern drawn in an Image, then TextureBrush is used. In the following example, an Image is loaded from the file, which is used to create TextureBrush. TextureBrush constructor takes other parameters like Wrapmode, which specifies how the Image is tiled, source and destination Rectangle, etc.

```
Image img = new Bitmap("flower.jpg");
TextureBrush textureBrush = new TextureBrush(img);
g.FillRectangle(textureBrush, new Rectangle(50, 50, 200, 200));
bmp.Save("textureBrush.png");
```

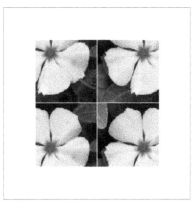

Figure 5-14. TextureBrush

LinearGradientBrush

To fill with gradients of different colors, LinearGradientBrush is used. LinearGradientBrush constructor takes two colors to create a gradient, a Rectangle, which is the size of the Brush, and LinearGradientMode, which determines the direction the gradient applies.

```
LinearGradientBrush linearGradientBrush =
new LinearGradientBrush(new Point(0, 0), new Point(200, 200),
Color.Black, Color.LightGray);
g.FillRectangle(linearGradientBrush, new Rectangle(25, 25, 150,
150));
bmp.Save("linearGradientBrush.png");
```

Figure 5-15. LinearGradientBrush

PathGradientBrush

PathGradientBrush applies gradients from outside to the center of the figure. The following example demonstrates the use of PathGradientBrush.

```
GraphicsPath graphicsPath = new GraphicsPath();
graphicsPath.AddRectangle(new Rectangle(0, 0, 200, 200));

PathGradientBrush pathGradientBrush = new
        PathGradientBrush(graphicsPath);

pathGradientBrush.CenterColor = Color.Black;

pathGradientBrush.SurroundColors = new Color[]
        { Color.LightGray };

g.FillRectangle(pathGradientBrush,
        new Rectangle(25, 25, 150, 150));

bmp.Save("pathGradientBrush.png");
```

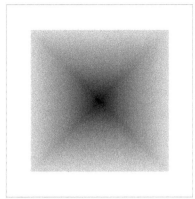

Figure 5-16. PathGradientBrush

Different Types of Brushes in WPF

SolidColorBrush

In WPF, SolidColorBrush is a class that represents a solid color brush used to paint an area with a solid color. It derives from the Brush class, the base class for all brushes in WPF. Below is an example.

```
Canvas canvas = new Canvas();
canvas.Measure(new Size(400, 400));
canvas.Background = Brushes.White;

Rectangle rectangle = new Rectangle();
rectangle.Width = 200;
rectangle.Height = 200;
rectangle.Stroke = new SolidColorBrush(Colors.Black);
rectangle.Fill = new SolidColorBrush(Colors.Gray);

Canvas.SetLeft(rectangle, 100);
Canvas.SetTop(rectangle, 100);
canvas.Children.Add(rectangle);
canvas.Arrange(new Rect(new Size(400, 400)));
```

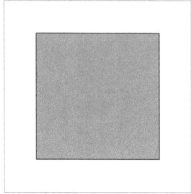

Figure 5-17. WPF-SolidColorBrush

LinearGradientBrush

The LinearGradientBrush class represents a brush that paints an area with a linear gradient. It smoothly transitions the color across the specified gradient vector.

```
Canvas canvas = new Canvas();
canvas.Measure(new Size(400, 400));
canvas.Background = Brushes.White;

LinearGradientBrush brush = new LinearGradientBrush();

brush.GradientStops.Add(new GradientStop(Colors.White, 0.0));
brush.GradientStops.Add(new GradientStop(Colors.Gray, 0.5));
brush.GradientStops.Add(new GradientStop(Colors.Black, 1.0));

Rectangle rectangle = new Rectangle();
rectangle.Width = 200;
rectangle.Height = 200;
rectangle.Fill = brush;

Canvas.SetLeft(rectangle, 100);
Canvas.SetTop(rectangle, 100);
canvas.Children.Add(rectangle);
canvas.Arrange(new Rect(new Size(400, 400)));
```

Here I defined three GradientStop objects within the Brush to specify the colors at different positions along the gradient. The GradientStop class represents a single color within the gradient. It takes two parameters: the color value and the offset. Here we added three gradient stops: white at offset 0.0, gray at offset 0.5, and black at offset 1.0.

Figure 5-18. WPF-LinearGradientBrush

RadialGradientBrush

The RadialGradientBrush class represents a brush that paints an area with a radial gradient. It creates a smooth transition of colors originating from a center point and radiating outward.

```
Canvas canvas = new Canvas();
canvas.Measure(new Size(400, 400));
canvas.Background = Brushes.White;

RadialGradientBrush brush = new RadialGradientBrush();

brush.GradientStops.Add(new GradientStop(Colors.White, 0.0));
brush.GradientStops.Add(new GradientStop(Colors.Gray, 0.5));
brush.GradientStops.Add(new GradientStop(Colors.Black, 1.0));

Rectangle rectangle = new Rectangle();
rectangle.Width = 200;
rectangle.Height = 200;
rectangle.Fill = brush;
```

```
Canvas.SetLeft(rectangle, 100);
Canvas.SetTop(rectangle, 100);
canvas.Children.Add(rectangle);
canvas.Arrange(new Rect(new Size(400, 400)));
```

The GradientStops can be added in the RadialGradientBrush to control the Brush precisely.

Figure 5-19. WPF-RadialGradientBrush

ImageBrush

The ImageBrush class represents a brush that paints an area with an Image. It allows you to use an Image as a fill for a shape or a background for a UI element.

```
Canvas canvas = new Canvas();
canvas.Measure(new Size(400, 400));
canvas.Background = Brushes.White;

Rectangle rectangle = new Rectangle();
rectangle.Width = 200;
rectangle.Height = 200;
rectangle.Fill =
    new ImageBrush(new BitmapImage(new Uri(@"flower.jpg",
    UriKind.RelativeOrAbsolute)));

Canvas.SetLeft(rectangle, 100);
Canvas.SetTop(rectangle, 100);
```

```
canvas.Children.Add(rectangle);
canvas.Arrange(new Rect(new Size(400, 400)));
```

The ImageSource property accepts an instance of the BitmapImage class, a WPF-specific class for handling Images. In this case, we create a new BitmapImage object and provide the URI of the Image file, which can be a relative or absolute path.

Figure 5-20. WPF-ImageBrush

DrawingBrush

In WPF, the DrawingBrush is a brush that defines its content as a drawing, allowing you to paint the background or fill a visual element with a complex or custom-drawn shape. It uses a Drawing object to define its content, including various shapes, lines, and other graphical elements. In the below example, I am filling a Rectangle with a text shape.

```
Canvas canvas = new Canvas();
canvas.Measure(new Size(400, 400));
canvas.Background = Brushes.White;

Rectangle rectangle = new Rectangle();
rectangle.Width = 200;
rectangle.Height = 200;

System.Windows.FontStyle fontStyle = FontStyles.Normal;
```

```
FontWeight fontWeight = FontWeights.Medium;

Typeface typeface =
    new Typeface(new FontFamily("Comic Sans MS"),
    fontStyle, fontWeight, FontStretches.Normal);

FormattedText formattedText =
    new FormattedText("Text", CultureInfo.GetCultureInfo("en-us"),
    FlowDirection.LeftToRight,
    typeface, 100, System.Windows.Media.Brushes.Black, 90);

Geometry textGeometry =
    formattedText.BuildGeometry(
    new System.Windows.Point(0, 0));

GeometryDrawing geometryDrawing =
    new GeometryDrawing(Brushes.Pink,
    new Pen(Brushes.Red, 5), textGeometry);

rectangle.Fill = new DrawingBrush(geometryDrawing);

Canvas.SetLeft(rectangle, 100);
Canvas.SetTop(rectangle, 100);
canvas.Children.Add(rectangle);
canvas.Arrange(new Rect(new Size(400, 400)));
```

Here a DrawingBrush is created from a text geometry and used as a fill Brush for the Rectangle. This allows us to fill one shape with another shape to create complex drawings.

Figure 5-21. WPF-DrawingBrush

Image With Transparency

This section is about System.Drawing.Color class. System.Drawing.Color contains Red, Blue, Green, and Alpha components. These components I can access through class properties, Color.R, Color.G, Color.B, and Color.A. You can create any color by changing these values. Values change from 0 to 255. 0 is low intensity, and 255 is the maximum intensity. 0 value for alpha means fully transparent, and 255 means fully opaque.

The following example demonstrates the use of transparent color. I am creating an Image containing a balloon with a transparent background. This Image is drawn four times, in different locations on another Image. Because the background of the Image containing a balloon shape is transparent, an output Image is created, as shown in Figure 5-22.

```
Point point = new Point(150, 150);

Bitmap balloonBmp = new Bitmap(300, 200);

Graphics balloonBmpGraphics =
    Graphics.FromImage(balloonBmp);
```

```
balloonBmpGraphics.SmoothingMode =
    SmoothingMode.AntiAlias;

balloonBmpGraphics.InterpolationMode =
        InterpolationMode.HighQualityBicubic;

balloonBmpGraphics.Clear(Color.Transparent);

GraphicsPath graphicsPath = new GraphicsPath();
graphicsPath.StartFigure();

graphicsPath.AddBezier(
    new Point(147, 152), new Point(290, 30),
    new Point(10, 30), new Point(152, 152));

graphicsPath.CloseFigure();

PathGradientBrush pathGradientBrush =
    new PathGradientBrush(graphicsPath);

pathGradientBrush.CenterColor = Color.Black;

pathGradientBrush.SurroundColors =
    new Color[] { Color.LightGray };

balloonBmpGraphics.FillRectangle(pathGradientBrush,
    new RectangleF(0, 0, 300, 200));

Pen pen = new Pen(Color.Black, 4);
balloonBmpGraphics.DrawPath(pen, graphicsPath);


Bitmap bmp = new Bitmap(300, 300);
Graphics g = Graphics.FromImage(bmp);

g.Clear(Color.Transparent);
g.DrawImage(balloonBmp, new Point(0, 0));
g.DrawImage(balloonBmp, new Point(50, 50));
g.DrawImage(balloonBmp, new Point(-50, +50));
g.DrawImage(balloonBmp, new Point(0, 100));
```

bmp.Save("Balloons.png");

The code

balloonBmpGraphics.Clear(Color.Transparent);

fills the balloonBmp Image with transparent color. So the balloon shape drawn on that Image has a transparent background. This allows me to draw a balloon to the target Image without a background.

Figure 5-22. Balloons with transparent background

Clipping an Image

Sometimes I need to cut a part of an Image and paste it on another Image or save that part as a separate Image. In the example below, I am clipping a small rectangular area from the source bitmap, copying it to the target bitmap, and saving it as a file.

```
Bitmap sourcebmp = new Bitmap("flower.jpg");
Rectangle sourceRectangle = new Rectangle(100, 100, 100, 100);
Rectangle targetRectangle = new Rectangle(0, 0, 100, 100);
Bitmap outputbmp = new Bitmap(100,100);
Graphics g = Graphics.FromImage(outputbmp);
```

```
g.DrawImage(sourcebmp, targetRectangle,
      sourceRectangle, GraphicsUnit.Pixel);

outputbmp.Save("cropedimage.png");
```

Clipping an Image in WPF

In WPF, you can clip an Image using the Clip property of the Image control. The Clip property takes an object of type Geometry. So I can use any type of Geometry object, such as RectangleGeometry, EllipseGeometry, PathGeometry, LineGeometry, and PolygonGeometry, to achieve different clipping shapes. In the below example, I am clipping an Image in the shape of a text.

```
Canvas canvas = new Canvas();
canvas.Measure(new Size(500, 500));
canvas.Background = Brushes.Transparent;

System.Windows.FontStyle fontStyle = FontStyles.Normal;
FontWeight fontWeight = FontWeights.Medium;

Typeface typeface =
   new Typeface(new FontFamily("Comic Sans MS"),
   fontStyle, fontWeight, FontStretches.Normal);

FormattedText formattedText =
   new FormattedText("Text", CultureInfo.GetCultureInfo("en-us"),
   FlowDirection.LeftToRight, typeface, 100,
   System.Windows.Media.Brushes.Black, 90);

Geometry textGeometry =
      formattedText.BuildGeometry(
      new System.Windows.Point(0, 0));

Image image = new Image();

image.Source = new BitmapImage(
   new Uri(@"flower.png", UriKind.RelativeOrAbsolute));
```

```
image.HorizontalAlignment = HorizontalAlignment.Left;
image.Clip = textGeometry;

Canvas.SetLeft(image, 50);
Canvas.SetTop(image, 50);

canvas.Children.Add(image);
canvas.Arrange(new Rect(new Size(500, 500)));
```

Figure 5-23. WPF-Clipping the Image in the text shape

Here I used the BuildGeometry method of FormattedText class to create the Geometry. So the Image is clipped in the shape of the text given.

Chapter 6

Project - Rotating Flower Animation

In this chapter, I am doing a full project explanation. Rotating flower animation is created in WPF and GDI+ as two separate projects. The project's output is a video of a rotating flower shape with colorful petals. Videos are created in 25 Frames per second and in full HD size. The full source code is given at the end of the section.

Download the source code of all projects/examples covered in this book at https://github.com/Jayasankar-S/CSharp-Animation-And-FFmpeg-Book

WPF Example

In WPF, PathFigure contains connected segments to define a figure. PathGeometry, which represents a complex shape, contains a collection of PathFigures. A PathFigure array is set as the Data property value of the Path object, and this Path object can be added to the Canvas.

Figure 6-1. Rotating Flower

Different flower petals are drawn using PolyQuadraticBezierSegment, a class inherited from PathSegment. The PolyQuadraticBezierSegment takes a PointCollection object as a parameter in the constructor. PointCollection contains 4 points which are the control points of the curve. The control points are aligned so the resulting path gets a petal shape. The petals of the flowers are created using PathGeometry class and filled with different colors, and RotateTransform class is used to draw all the petals at different angles. The Image-by-Image angle of all petals was slightly changed to create an effect of rotation.

Creating the Petal

To create a Path object representing a flower petal, the GetFlowerPetalPath() function is called with some relative points as parameters. These control points create a Bezier curve that looks like a petal.

```
Path flowerPetal =GetFlowerPetalPath( new Point(0, 0),
        new Point(-200, 450), new Point(0, 440),
        new Point(200, 450), brushes[j]);
```

The GetFlowerPetalPath method returns a Path object which represents a flower petal shape filled with the color of the Brush object passed as a parameter. Following is the picture (Figure 6-2) of the first petal, and the first color used is DarkMagenta.

Figure 6-2. Petal was created using Path

Below is the full code of the GetFlowerPetalPath method.

```
private Path GetFlowerPetalPath(Point point1, Point point2,
        Point point3, Point point4, Brush brush)
{
    // Creating a Bezier curve using points given.
    PointCollection pointCollection =
        new PointCollection { point2, point3, point4, point1 };

    PolyQuadraticBezierSegment polyQuadraticBezierSegment =
        new PolyQuadraticBezierSegment(pointCollection,
        false);

    // PathFigure is created, and adding
    // PolyQuadraticBezierSegment to it.
    PathFigure pathFigure = new PathFigure();
```

```
pathFigure.StartPoint = point1;
pathFigure.Segments.Add(polyQuadraticBezierSegment);
pathFigure.IsClosed = true;
Path path = new Path();

//Brush to fill color.
path.Fill = brush;

// Adding PathFigure to Path
path.Data = new PathGeometry(new PathFigure[]
    { pathFigure });

return path;
}
```

Figure 6-3 shows the control points and the curves created. To create a PolyQuadraticBezierSegment object, I must provide each quadratic Bezier curve's control points and endpoints. For every three points in the collection, the first and second points specify the two control points that determine the shape of the curve, and the third point specifies the endpoint. Here four points are given, which results in two curves.

```
PointCollection pointCollection =
    new PointCollection { point2, point3, point4, point1 };

PolyQuadraticBezierSegment polyQuadraticBezierSegment =
    new PolyQuadraticBezierSegment(pointCollection, false);
```

The first curve is the result of point1, which is (0, 0), point2, which is (-200, 450); and point3, which is (0, 440). But if you look into the PointCollection object, I passed four points, point2, point3, point4, point1. So the starting point for the first curve is missing. The PolyQuadraticBezierSegment object will take the StartPoint of the PathFigure as the first point. So I do not need to specify the first point. It is taken automatically from the PathFigure. So the first curve starts at point1 (0, 0) and ends at point3 (0, 440). The point2 (-200, 450) is the control point, which acts like a magnet bending the line between point 1 and point 3. The second curve is the result of points point3, which is (0, 440); point4, which is (200,

450); and point1, which is (0, 0). The second curve starts at the endpoint of the previous curve. So the second curve starts at point3. The point4 is the control point acting as a magnet that bends the line.

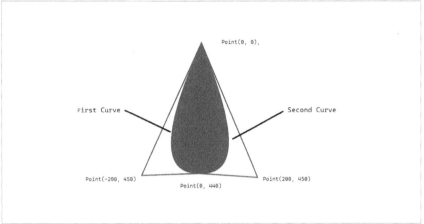

Figure 6-3. Control Points and Curves

I have to draw nine petals with equal angular distance from one another to create a flower. So each petal is drawn on canvas with different colors and rotated 40 degrees to get a flower-like shape. See the below code.

```
for (int j = 0; j < 9; j++)
{
    Path flowerPetal = GetFlowerPetalPath( ... );

    flowerPetal.RenderTransform =
        new RotateTransform((40 * j), 0, 0);

    Canvas.SetLeft(flowerPetal, 900);
    Canvas.SetTop(flowerPetal, 500);

    canvas.Children.Add(flowerPetal);
}
```

The origin of flowerPetal is set by static methods Canvas.SetLeft and Canvas.SetTop. Each petal is rotated 40 degrees more than the previous one in each iteration to create a flower shape, as shown in Figure 6-1.

Now a flower was created. I need to rotate it to create the animation. One Image is created per iteration of the loop. Here I am creating 1000 Images. I am adding a rotation to the petals using the angleIncrement variable. The angleIncrement starts with the value of one and increases by the value of one in each iteration. So all flower petals rotated one degree more than in the previous Image. When converted to video with 25 frames per second, every second, the flower rotates by 25 degrees. So each petal is rotated 40 degrees to create the flower, plus the angleIncrement value to create the rotating flower. See the below code.

```
int angleIncrement = 1;
for (int i = 0; i < 1000; i++) // loop for creating Images
{
        ....................

        for (int j = 0; j < 9; j++) //loop for drawing petals
        {
           Path flowerPetal = GetFlowerPetalPath( ... );

           flowerPetal.RenderTransform =
                new RotateTransform(angleIncrement+(40 * j), 0, 0);
           ....................
        }

        ....................
        pngBitmapEncoder.Save(fileStream);// saving the Image
        angleIncrement++;
}

CreateVideoFromImages("D:\\ffmpeg\\",
        "D:\\ffmpeg\\Rotating Flower.mp4");
```

The full code of this project is given below.

Full Code

```csharp
using System;
using System.Diagnostics;
using System.Windows;
using System.Windows.Controls;
using System.Windows.Media;
using System.Windows.Media.Imaging;
using System.Windows.Shapes;

public void CreateVideo()
{
    if (!System.IO.Directory.Exists("ImageOutput"))
        System.IO.Directory.CreateDirectory("ImageOutput");

    if (!System.IO.Directory.Exists("VideoOutput"))
        System.IO.Directory.CreateDirectory("VideoOutput");

    Brush[] brushes = new Brush[]
    {
        Brushes.DarkMagenta,
        Brushes.DarkSalmon,
        Brushes.DarkOliveGreen,
        Brushes.Gray,
        Brushes.Lime,
        Brushes.LightCoral,
        Brushes.SpringGreen,
        Brushes.Yellow,
        Brushes.Pink,
        Brushes.GreenYellow
    };

    int angleIncrement = 1;

    for (int i = 0; i < 1000; i++)
    {
        Canvas canvas = new Canvas();
        canvas.Measure(new Size(1920, 1080));
        canvas.Background = Brushes.White;

        for (int j = 0; j < 9; j++)
        {
            Path flowerPetal =
                GetFlowerPetalPath(
                new Point(0, 0),
```

```
        new Point(-200, 450),
        new Point(0, 440),
        new Point(200, 450), brushes[j]);

    flowerPetal.RenderTransform =
        new RotateTransform(angleIncrement + (40 * j), 0, 0);

    Canvas.SetLeft(flowerPetal, 900);
    Canvas.SetTop(flowerPetal, 500);

    // Adding petals to canvas
    canvas.Children.Add(flowerPetal);
}

// Arranging the children in Canvas.
canvas.Arrange(new Rect(new Size(1920, 1080)));

string imageName = ("000000000" + i.ToString());

imageName = imageName.Substring(
    imageName.Length - 6, 6) + ".png";

RenderTargetBitmap renderTargetBitmap =
    new RenderTargetBitmap(1920, 1080, 96, 96,
    PixelFormats.Pbgra32);

renderTargetBitmap.Render(canvas);

System.IO.FileStream fileStream =
    new System.IO.FileStream(
    System.IO.Path.GetFullPath(
    "ImageOutput\\" + imageName),
    System.IO.FileMode.Create);

PngBitmapEncoder pngBitmapEncoder =
        new PngBitmapEncoder();

pngBitmapEncoder.Frames.Add(
    BitmapFrame.Create(renderTargetBitmap));

pngBitmapEncoder.Save(fileStream);
fileStream.Close();

//angleIncrement increases by one after each Image creation.
angleIncrement++;
}


CreateVideoFromImages(
```

```
                System.IO.Path.GetFullPath("ImageOutput\\"),
                System.IO.Path.GetFullPath(
                "VideoOutput\\Rotating Flower.mp4"));
}



private Path GetFlowerPetalPath(Point point1, Point point2,
                Point point3, Point point4, Brush brush)
{
    // Creating a Bezier curve using points given.
    PointCollection pointCollection =
            new PointCollection { point2, point3, point4, point1 };
    PolyQuadraticBezierSegment polyQuadraticBezierSegment =
            new PolyQuadraticBezierSegment(pointCollection, false);

    // PathFigure is created, and adding PolyQuadraticBezierSegment to it.
    PathFigure pathFigure = new PathFigure();
    pathFigure.StartPoint = point1;
    pathFigure.Segments.Add(polyQuadraticBezierSegment);
    pathFigure.IsClosed = true;
    Path path = new Path();

    //Brush to fill color.
    path.Fill = brush;

    // Adding PathFigure to Path
    path.Data = new PathGeometry(new PathFigure[] { pathFigure });
    return path;
}

public static void CreateVideoFromImages(
    string inputImagesfolder, string videoOutputFile)
{
    Process process = new Process();
    process.StartInfo.FileName = "cmd.exe";

    process.StartInfo.Arguments = "/C " + " ffmpeg -i \"" +
        inputImagesfolder +
        "%06d.png\" -y -pix_fmt yuv420p \""
        + videoOutputFile + "\" ";

    process.StartInfo.UseShellExecute = false;
    process.Start();
    process.WaitForExit();

    int exitCode = process.ExitCode;
    if (exitCode == 0)
    {
```

```
    Console.WriteLine("Creating Video From" +
    " Images completed successfully!");
  }
  else
  {
    Console.WriteLine($"FFmpeg processing " +
    $"failed with exit code: {exitCode}");
  }
}
```

GDI+ Example

Rotating flower animation project I am rewriting using GDI+ code. As in the WPF example, the output of this project is a video of a flower with colorful petals rotating based on its center. The same concept as in the earlier example is used here. Instead of the WPF Path object, I am using GraphicsPath class.

The GetFlowerPetalPath method below returns a GraphicsPath object containing a Bezier curve. The AddBezier Method of GraphicsPath class adds a Bezier curve to the GraphicsPath object. The AddBezier method takes four points as parameters. The first and last parameters are starting and endpoints of the curve. The second and third parameters are control points which bend the line between starting and end points to create a curve.

```
graphicsPath.AddBezier(
                new Point(0, 0),
                new Point(-200, 450),
                new Point(200, 450),
                new Point(0, 0));
```

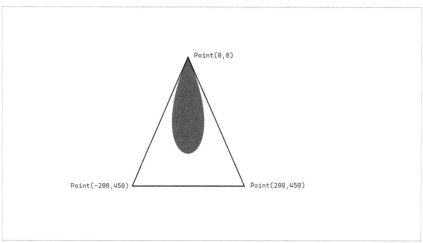

Figure 6-4. Control Points and Curves (GDI+)

```
static private GraphicsPath GetFlowerPetalPath()
{
        GraphicsPath graphicsPath = new GraphicsPath();
        graphics path.StartFigure();

        graphics path.AddBezier(
                new Point(0, 0),
                new Point(-200, 450),
                new Point(200, 450),
                new Point(0, 0));

        graphics path.CloseFigure();
        return graphicsPath;
}
```

The graphics object origin is moved to the middle of the Image using the code.

g.TranslateTransform(1920 / 2, 1080 / 2);

The flowerPetal object is drawn nine times with different color brushes, and after drawing, each petal graphics object's coordinates are rotated by 40 degrees to add an angular distance between petals. So nine petals are drawn from the origin, which is the center of the Image, and at an angular distance of 40 degrees from the nearby petal.

```
GraphicsPath flowerPetal = GetFlowerPetalPath();
for (int j = 0; j < 9; j++)
{
    g.FillPath(brushes[j], flowerPetal);
    g.RotateTransform(40);
}
```

Each Image is created per iteration of the loop. Here I am creating 1000 Images. I am adding a rotation to the flower using the angleIncrement variable. The angleIncrement starts with the value of one and increases by a value of one per iteration. So all flower petals rotated one degree more than in the previous Image. When converted to video with 25 frames per second, every second flower rotates 25 degrees. So each petal is rotated 40 degrees to create the flower, plus the angleIncrement value to create the rotating flower. See the below code.

```
int angleIncrement = 1;

for (int i = 0; i < 1000; i++) // loop for creating Images
{
    ......................

    g.TranslateTransform(1920 / 2, 1080 / 2);
    g.RotateTransform(angleIncrement);
    GraphicsPath flowerPetal = GetFlowerPetalPath();

    for (int j = 0; j < 9; j++)
    {
        g.FillPath(brushes[j], flowerPetal);
        g.RotateTransform(40);

    }
    ......................
```

```
        angleIncrement++;
    }
```

Full Code

```csharp
using System;
using System.Diagnostics;
using System.Drawing;
using System.Drawing.Drawing2D;
using System.IO;

 static Brush[] brushes = new Brush[]
{
     Brushes.DarkMagenta,
     Brushes.DarkSalmon,
     Brushes.DarkOliveGreen,
     Brushes.Gray,
     Brushes.Lime,
     Brushes.LightCoral,
     Brushes.SpringGreen,
     Brushes.Yellow,
     Brushes.Pink,
     Brushes.GreenYellow
};

public static void CreateVideo()
{
   if (!System.IO.Directory.Exists("ImageOutput"))
     System.IO.Directory.CreateDirectory("ImageOutput");

   if (!System.IO.Directory.Exists("VideoOutput"))
     System.IO.Directory.CreateDirectory("VideoOutput");


   int angleIncrement = 1;
   for (int i = 0; i < 1000; i++)
   {
     Bitmap bmp = new Bitmap(1920, 1080);
     Graphics g = Graphics.FromImage(bmp);
     g.SmoothingMode = SmoothingMode.AntiAlias;
     g.PixelOffsetMode = PixelOffsetMode.HighQuality;
     g.CompositingQuality = CompositingQuality.HighQuality;
     g.InterpolationMode = InterpolationMode.HighQualityBilinear;
     g.PageUnit = GraphicsUnit.Pixel;

     g.Clear(Color.White);
```

```
        g.TranslateTransform(1920 / 2, 1080 / 2);
        g.RotateTransform(angleIncrement);
        GraphicsPath flowerPetal = GetFlowerPetalPath();

        for (int j = 0; j < 9; j++)
        {
            g.FillPath(brushes[j], flowerPetal);
            g.RotateTransform(40);
        }

        string imageName = ("000000000" + i.ToString());
        imageName = imageName.Substring(
            imageName.Length - 6, 6) + ".png";

        bmp.Save(Path.GetFullPath(
            "ImageOutput\\" + imageName));
        Console.WriteLine("Created Image " + imageName);
        angleIncrement++;

    }

    CreateVideoFromImages(
        System.IO.Path.GetFullPath("ImageOutput\\"),
        System.IO.Path.GetFullPath(
        "VideoOutput\\Rotating Flower.mp4"));
}


static private GraphicsPath GetFlowerPetalPath()
{
    GraphicsPath graphicsPath = new GraphicsPath();
    graphicsPath.StartFigure();
    graphicsPath.AddBezier(
            new Point(0, 0),
            new Point(-200, 450),
            new Point(200, 450),
            new Point(0, 0));
    graphicsPath.CloseFigure();
    return graphicsPath;
}


public static void CreateVideoFromImages(
  string inputImagesfolder,
  string videoOutputFile)
{
    Process process = new Process();
    process.StartInfo.FileName = "cmd.exe";
```

```
process.StartInfo.Arguments = "/C " + " ffmpeg -i \"" +
    inputImagesfolder +
    "%06d.png\" -y -pix_fmt yuv420p \""
    + videoOutputFile + "\" ";

process.StartInfo.UseShellExecute = false;
process.Start();
process.WaitForExit();

int exitCode = process.ExitCode;
if (exitCode == 0)
{
    Console.WriteLine("Creating Video From" +
        " Images completed successfully!");
}
else
{
    Console.WriteLine($"FFmpeg processing " +
        $"failed with exit code: {exitCode}");
}
}
```

Chapter 7

Project - Rainbow Animation

The rainbow has seven colors. Starting from violet in the inner layer to red in the outside layer. Each layer is in the form of an arc. So I can draw a rainbow using seven arcs, one drawn above another in appropriate colors. Here I am creating a rainbow drawing animation video. The video starts with the violet arc, and one by one, other color arcs are completed, and at the end, a full rainbow is drawn. I am explaining both GDI+ and WPF examples in detail below.

Download the source code of all projects/examples covered in this book at https://github.com/Jayasankar-S/CSharp-Animation-And-FFmpeg-Book

WPF Example

In WPF ArcSegment is used to construct an arc. The ArcSegment class is complicated compared to System.Drawing.Arc class. The following figures show the different stages of the animation. Finally, seven arcs are drawn to complete a full rainbow.

Figure 7-1. Rainbow animation screenshot

Figure 7-2. Rainbow animation screenshot

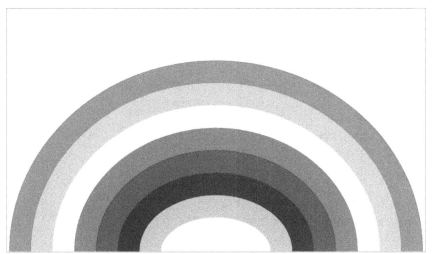

Figure 7-3. Rainbow animation screenshot

AddArc method

Following is the full code of the AddArc method.

```
private void AddArc(Canvas canvas, Brush brush,
            Point arcCentre, Size size,
            int arcThickness, Double percentage)
{
    double xRadius = size.Width;
    double yRadius = size.Height;

    double angle = (180 * percentage / 100) - 180;

    double x = arcCentre.X +
        Math.Cos(angle * Math.PI / 180) * xRadius;

    double y = arcCentre.Y +
        Math.Sin(angle * Math.PI / 180) * yRadius;

    ArcSegment arcSegment =
        new ArcSegment(new Point(x, y),
        size, 0, false, SweepDirection.Clockwise,
```

```
    true);

    PathFigure pathFigure = new PathFigure();
    pathFigure.StartPoint =
        new Point(arcCentre.X - size.Width, arcCentre.Y);
    pathFigure.Segments.Add(arcSegment);

    Path path = new Path();
    path.Stroke = brush;
    path.StrokeThickness = arcThickness;

    path.Data = new PathGeometry(
        new PathFigure[] { pathFigure });

    canvas.Children.Add(path);
}
```

The AddArc method is the core part of this project. The AddArc method adds a Path object containing arc figures to the Canvas. The first parameter passed to the AddArc method is the Canvas object, where the arc is to be added. The size of the canvas is 1920 x 1080. The next parameter is the stroke brush to draw the arc. The third parameter, the arcCenter, represents the center of the arc. Here the arc center is always the middle of the bottom side of the Canvas, which is the point (960, 1080). The fourth parameter is the thickness of the arc which is set to the Path object by the following code.

```
path.StrokeThickness = arcThickness;
```

The fifth parameter is the percentage of arc to be drawn. In the animation, Arc's angle starts from zero and increases Image by Image to 180 degrees. Then the next arc is drawn, and so on. So the percentage parameter determines the percentage of the arc angle completed. Zero percentage means zero degree drawn, and a hundred percent means 180 degrees completed.

```
double angle = (180 * percentage / 100)-180;
```

In the above line, 180 degrees is subtracted because the arc starts at -180 degrees (or 270 degrees) and ends at 0 degrees. The percentage is converted to an angle in degrees, and the angle is converted to x, and y coordinate values using the Ellipse equation, which will be a point in the Ellipse outline.

```
double x = arcCentre.X +
      Math.Cos(angle * Math.PI / 180) * xRadius;

double y = arcCentre.Y +
      Math.Sin(angle * Math.PI / 180) * yRadius;
```

The arcCentre.X and the arcCentre.Y are added in the above equation to shift the arc origin or center of the arc to the arcCentre point. Otherwise, an arc is drawn around the point (0,0).

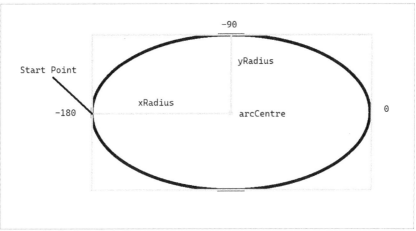

Figure 7-4. Arc details

Next ArcSegment object is created using the following code.

```
ArcSegment arcSegment =
  new ArcSegment(
  new Point(x,y), size, 0, false, SweepDirection.Clockwise, true);
```

The ArcSegment class is a little bit difficult to understand. GDI+ Graphics DrawArc or FillArc method takes a Rectangle object, startAngle, and sweepAngle as parameters. The arc starts at the start angle and is drawn up to an angular distance of sweep angle. This GDI+ way of drawing arcs is simple, but in the case of ArcSegment, the arc is drawn from point to point. In the ArcSegment constructor, I specify the end-point only, and the start point is taken from the PathFigure object's start point. The second parameter of the ArcSegment constructor is the size. Size specifies the horizontal and vertical radius of the arc. The third parameter is the rotation angle, which I can set to zero. If I specify a value other than zero to the rotation angle, the Ellipse to which the arc belongs will be rotated by that many degrees. Below is the picture(Figure 7-5) of the same arcs; the only difference is that one arc is rotated 90 degrees.

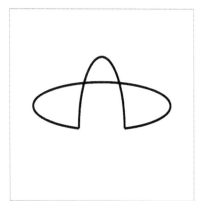

Figure 7-5. The same arc with different rotation angles

The fourth parameter of the ArcSegment constructor is the isLargeArc, bool type. The fifth parameter is sweep direction. Four arcs are possible from two points if the size, start point, end point, and rotation angle are constant. One small arc and one large arc can be drawn clockwise. One small arc and one large arc can also be drawn counterclockwise. The below pictures show four possible ways of creating arcs when size, start point, end point, and rotation angle are constant.

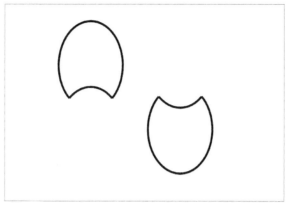

Figure 7-6. Four arcs drawn between the same points

AddRainbow method

The DrawArc method adds an arc to the canvas. The AddRainbow method uses the DrawArc method to add seven arcs in seven colors to create a rainbow. Inner arcs are drawn first. Below is the full code of the AddRainbow method.

```
private void AddRainbow(Canvas canvas, Brush[] brushes,
    int arcNumber, double currentArcPercentage,
    int canvasWidth, int canvasHeight)
{
    Size arcSize;
    int initialXRadius = 300;
    int initialYRadius = 200;
    int arcThickness = 100;

    for (int j = 0; j < arcNumber; j++)
    {
        arcSize = new Size(
            initialXRadius + (j * arcThickness),
            initialYRadius + (j * arcThickness));
```

```
    AddArc(canvas, brushes[j],
        new Point(canvasWidth / 2, canvasHeight),
        arcSize, arcThickness, arcThickness);
}

arcSize = new Size(
    initialXRadius + (arcNumber * arcThickness),
    initialYRadius + (arcNumber * arcThickness));

AddArc(canvas, brushes[arcNumber],
    new Point(canvasWidth / 2, canvasHeight),
    arcSize, arcThickness, currentArcPercentage);
}
```

In the animation, initially, the violet arc starts from -180 degrees, and Image by Image, its angle increases and reaches 0 degrees. Next starts the indigo arc. The Indigo arc is also drawn from -180 to 0 in 8 seconds. One important thing to notice is that, while drawing the indigo arc, the violet arc is already present there, and it will be 100 percent drawn. Similarly, when I draw a red arc which is the last one, all the other arcs will be drawn 100 percent.

```
Size arcSize;
int initialXRadius = 300;
int initialYRadius = 200;
int arcThickness = 100;
```

The arcSize is the xRadius and yRadius of the arc. The arc size of the indigo arc is bigger than the violet arc. Below is the arc size calculating logic.

```
arcSize = new Size(initialXRadius + (arcNumber * arcThickness),
                initialYRadius + (arcNumber * arcThickness));
```

The initialXRadius and initialYRadius are the x and y radius of the violet arc. When I draw the next arc, which is an indigo arc, the x radius and y radius should be increased by arc thickness. Then a bigger arc in indigo color is drawn above the violet arc. For each arc drawn afterward, the x and y radius will be increased by arcThickness, which is 100. Look at Figure 7-2. You can see four arcs there. Violet, indigo, and blue are completed and in 100 percent. The green arc is partially completed. To draw that picture, the arcNumber value used is 3. So three arcs completed 100 percent, and the fourth arc, which is green, uses the currentArcPercentage value to determine the angle to draw.

```
//If the arcNumber value is 3, violet, indigo, and blue are drawn in
100 percentage
for (int j = 0; j < arcNumber; j++)
{
    arcSize = ...

  AddArc(canvas, brushes[j],
    new Point(canvasWidth / 2, canvasHeight),
    arcSize, arcThickness, 100);
}

arcSize = ...

// green arc drawn partially depends upon the value of
// currentArcPercentage.
AddArc(canvas, brushes[arcNumber],
    new Point(canvasWidth / 2, canvasHeight),
    arcSize, arcThickness, currentArcPercentage);
```

SaveCanvasToImage Method

The SaveCanvasToImage method saves the Canvas as an Image. Below is the code.

```
private static void SaveCanvasToImage(
    Canvas canvas, int canvasWidth, int canvasHeight,
    int imageIndex, string outputFolder)
{
    canvas.Arrange(
        new Rect(new Size(canvasWidth, canvasHeight)));

    string imageName =
        ("000000000" + imageIndex.ToString());
```

```
imageName =
    imageName.Substring(imageName.Length - 6, 6) +
    ".png";

RenderTargetBitmap renderTargetBitmap =
    new RenderTargetBitmap(canvasWidth,
    canvasHeight, 96, 96, PixelFormats.Pbgra32);

renderTargetBitmap.Render(canvas);

System.IO.FileStream fileStream =
    new System.IO.FileStream(outputFolder + imageName,
    System.IO.FileMode.Create);

PngBitmapEncoder pngBitmapEncoder =
    new PngBitmapEncoder();

pngBitmapEncoder.Frames.Add(
    BitmapFrame.Create(renderTargetBitmap));

pngBitmapEncoder.Save(fileStream);

Console.WriteLine("Created Image " + imageName);
fileStream.Close();
canvas.Children.Clear();
}
```

Creating Rainbow Animation

Below is the code for creating the Rainbow animation.

```
public void CreateVideo()
{
    Brush[] brushes = new Brush[]
    {
        Brushes.Violet,
        Brushes.Indigo,
        Brushes.Blue,
        Brushes.Green,
```

```
    Brushes.Yellow,
    Brushes.Orange,
    Brushes.Red,
};

int arcNumber = 0;
Double currentArcPercentage = 0;
int canvasWidth = 1920;
int canvasHeight = 1080;

if (!System.IO.Directory.Exists("ImageOutput"))
    System.IO.Directory.CreateDirectory("ImageOutput");

if (!System.IO.Directory.Exists("VideoOutput"))
    System.IO.Directory.CreateDirectory("VideoOutput");

int imageCount = 0;
Canvas canvas = new Canvas();
canvas.Measure(new Size(canvasWidth, canvasHeight));

while (true)
{
    canvas.Background = Brushes.White;

    if (currentArcPercentage > 100)
    {
        currentArcPercentage = 0;
        arcNumber++;

        if (arcNumber >= 7)
            break;
    }

    AddRainbow(canvas, brushes, arcNumber,
        currentArcPercentage,
        canvasWidth, canvasHeight);

    SaveCanvasToImage(canvas, canvasWidth,
        canvasHeight, imageCount, "ImageOutput\\");
```

```
    currentArcPercentage =
        currentArcPercentage + 0.5;
    imageCount++;
  }

  CreateVideoFromImages("ImageOutput\\",
    "VideoOutput\\Rainbow.mp4");
}
```

A canvas is created with a width of 1920 and a height of 1080. In the while loop currentArcPercentage value and imageCount value increases after each iteration.

```
 currentArcPercentage = currentArcPercentage + 0.5;
 imageCount++;
```

The following code changes the arcNumber if the currentArcPercentage goes more than 100. So once one arc is completed arcNumber increases, and the next arc will start drawing. AddRainbow methods draw the rainbow using arcNumber and currentArcPercentage. The SaveCanvasToImage method saves the canvas contents to an Image file with Image count as the file name. Also, when the arcNumber value reaches seven, the loop exits and Images are converted to video using the CreateVideoFromImages method.

```
if (currentArcPercentage > 100)
{
    currentArcPercentage = 0;
    arcNumber++;
    if (arcNumber >= 7)
       break;
}
```

GDI+ Example

The GDI+ example follows the same logic as the above-discussed code. In GDI+ DrawArc method of Graphics class is used to draw an arc. The DrawArc method is simpler than using ArcSegment class in WPF. DrawArc method draws an arc with dimensions, thickness, and color at a specified point.

DrawArc method of Graphics class

DrawArc(Pen pen, Rectangle rect, Single startAngle, Single sweepAngle)

DrawArc method takes four parameters (I am explaining the overloaded function, which is used in our code. Other overloads are similar), a Pen object, a Rectangle object, which contains the information about the drawing point of the arc, x diameter, and y diameter. The next parameter is startAngle, the angle at which the arc starts. The arc I am drawing for the rainbow starts at 180 degrees (or -180 degrees). The next parameter is the sweepAngle. The sum of the startAngle and the sweepAngle specifies the end angle of the arc. In our case, startAngle is 180 degrees, and sweepAngle is 180 degrees. So the arc starts at 180 degrees and ends at 360 degrees(or 0 degrees).

AddRainbow method

The AddRainbow method follows exactly similar logic in the WPF example. Below is the code.

```
private static void AddRainbow(
    Graphics g, Pen[] pens, int bitmapWidth,
    int bitmapHeight, int arcThickness,
    int arcNumber, double currentArcPercentage)
{
    Size arcSize;
    int initialXRadius = 300;
    int initialYRadius = 200;

    for (int j = 0; j < arcNumber; j++)
    {
        arcSize = new Size(initialXRadius +
            (j * arcThickness * 2),
            initialYRadius + (j * arcThickness * 2));
```

```
        g.DrawArc(pens[j],
           new Rectangle(
              new Point((bitmapWidth - arcSize.Width) / 2,
              bitmapHeight - (arcSize.Height) / 2),
              arcSize), 180, 180);
     }

     arcSize = new Size(
        initialXRadius + (arcNumber * arcThickness * 2),
        initialYRadius + (arcNumber * arcThickness * 2));

     g.DrawArc(pens[arcNumber],
        new Rectangle(new Point((bitmapWidth - arcSize.Width) / 2,
              bitmapHeight - (arcSize.Height) / 2),
              arcSize),180,
              ((180 * (float)currentArcPercentage) / 100));
  }
```

The initialXRadius and initialYRadius are the x and y radius of the violet arc. The width of the arcSize represents the x diameter of the arc, and the height of the arcSize represents the y diameter. There is a difference between the arc size of the WPF example and this example. In the WPF example, arcSize represents the x radius and y radius. Here the calculation of arcSize changes accordingly.

Creating Rainbow Animation

Below is the code for creating the Rainbow animation.

```
public void CreateVideo()
{
   if (!System.IO.Directory.Exists("ImageOutput"))
      System.IO.Directory.CreateDirectory("ImageOutput");

   if (!System.IO.Directory.Exists("VideoOutput"))
      System.IO.Directory.CreateDirectory("VideoOutput");

   int bitmapWidth = 1920;
```

```
int bitmapheight = 1080;
int arcThickness = 100;

Pen[] pens = new Pen[]
{
    new Pen(Color.Violet,arcThickness),
    new Pen(Color.Indigo,arcThickness),
    new Pen(Color.Blue,arcThickness),
    new Pen(Color.Green,arcThickness),
    new Pen(Color.Yellow,arcThickness),
    new Pen(Color.Orange,arcThickness),
    new Pen(Color.Red,arcThickness),
};

Bitmap bmp =
    new Bitmap(bitmapWidth, bitmapheight);

Graphics g = Graphics.FromImage(bmp);
g.SmoothingMode = SmoothingMode.AntiAlias;

g.PixelOffsetMode = PixelOffsetMode.HighQuality;

g.CompositingQuality =
    CompositingQuality.HighQuality;

g.InterpolationMode =
    InterpolationMode.HighQualityBilinear;

g.PageUnit = GraphicsUnit.Pixel;

int arcNumber = 0;
Double currentArcPercentage = 0;
int imageCount = 0;

while (true)
{
    g.Clear(Color.White);

    AddRainbow(g, pens, bitmapWidth, bitmapheight,
        arcThickness, arcNumber, currentArcPercentage);
```

```
        if (currentArcPercentage > 100)
        {
           currentArcPercentage = 0;
           arcNumber++;
           if (arcNumber >= 7)
              break;
        }

        string imageName = ("000000000" +
                 imageCount.ToString());

        imageName =
           imageName.Substring(imageName.Length - 6, 6) +
           ".png";

        bmp.Save(Path.GetFullPath("ImageOutput\\" +
                 imageName));

        Console.WriteLine("Created Image " +
                 imageName);

        currentArcPercentage =
           currentArcPercentage + 0.5;

        imageCount++;
     }

   CreateVideoFromImages("ImageOutput\\",
      "VideoOutput\\Rainbow.mp4");

}
```

The AddRainbow draws arcs to the Image based on the arcNumber and the currentArcPercentage values. The Save method of the Bitmap class saves the canvas contents to an Image file with Image count as the file name. Also, when the arcNumber value reaches seven, the loop exits and Images are converted to video using the CreateVideoFromImages method.

Chapter 8

Project - 3D animation

WPF is a framework for building desktop applications in Windows. At the same time, WPF provides various animation capabilities, such as basic animations, keyframe animations, and storyboard animations. However, I can create 3D effects and animations in WPF by leveraging the power of DirectX by using the Viewport3D element. The Viewport3D provides a 3D rendering surface that allows you to define and display 3D content in your WPF application.

The basic requirements for creating a 3D animation are an object, a light source, and a camera. Objects can be created with 3D geometrical objects or MeshGeometry3D. MeshGeometry3D takes three-dimensional points. I can easily create a 3D object using the mesh logic, giving three mesh points representing the object's surface. A light source can be created with the DirectionalLight class. The light source can be placed in a three-dimensional point, and the Direction property decides to which direction the light source should point to illuminate the object. Next is the camera object, which views the object and surroundings. The PerspectiveCamera class is used for creating the camera. Like a light source, a camera object can be placed at a point and set in the direction the camera is pointing. The output Image we see in the canvas is the view of the object and its surroundings from the camera.

When I create a three-dimensional animation, I can create movements by changing the object's location, the points inside the mesh, the position and direction of the light source, the position and direction of the camera, etc. I can use different materials to wrap the object and also different colors. I can also set the color of the light source. Like in two-dimensional animation, I create a canvas, and the view from the camera is drawn to the canvas. Then I can convert the canvas to Image files, which are converted to video using FFmpeg.

Download the source code of all projects/examples covered in this book at https://github.com/Jayasankar-S/CSharp-Animation-And-FFmpeg-Book

Creating a Simple 3D Triangle Animation

As I said earlier, the basic things required to create an animation are an object, a light source, and a camera. Here I am explaining about creating a simple rotating 3D triangle animation. The following figures show the different stages of the triangle 3D animation. A triangle is drawn, and that triangle is rotated along the y-axis.

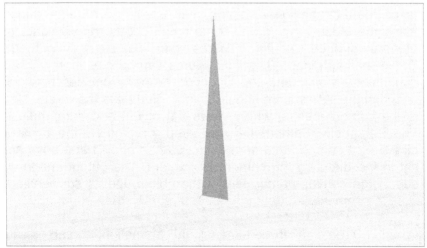

Figure 8-1. Rotating 3D triangle animation screenshot

Figure 8-2. Rotating 3D triangle animation screenshot

Figure 8-3. Rotating 3D triangle animation screenshot

Figure 8-4. Rotating 3D triangle animation screenshot

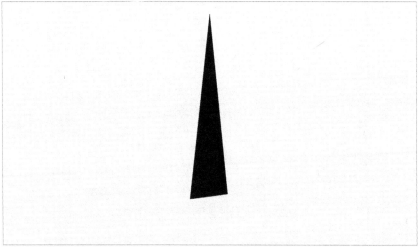

Figure 8-5. Rotating 3D triangle animation screenshot

Creating the Shape

To create a 3D triangle, I am using MeshGeometry3D class. The MeshGeometry3D objects take a minimum of three points to make a surface. I have to give points that count as a multiple of three. If I give six points, then the MeshGeometry3D class creates two surfaces, one with the first three points and the second one with the next three points. Here three points are given to create a triangle shape.

The CreateMeshGeometry method creates a MeshGeometry3D object which represents a three-dimensional triangle.

```
private static MeshGeometry3D CreateMeshGeometry()
{
    MeshGeometry3D myMeshGeometry3D =
                    new MeshGeometry3D();

    Point3DCollection myPositionCollection =
                    new Point3DCollection();

    myPositionCollection.Add(new Point3D(-0.5, 0, -0.5));
    myPositionCollection.Add(new Point3D(0.5, 0, 0.5));
    myPositionCollection.Add(new Point3D(0, 1.5, 0));
    myMeshGeometry3D.Positions = myPositionCollection;

    // Create a collection of triangle indices for MeshGeometry3D.
    Int32Collection myTriangleIndicesCollection =
                    new Int32Collection(new int[] { 0, 1, 2 });

    myMeshGeometry3D.TriangleIndices =
                    myTriangleIndicesCollection;

    return myMeshGeometry3D;
}
```

The code,

```
myMeshGeometry3D.Positions = myPositionCollection;
```

Sets the positions of the vertex. Here I used the points (-0.5, 0, -0.5), (0.5, 0, 0.5), and (0, 1.5, 0) as positions, which are the coordinates of a triangle in three-dimensional geometry.

The code

```
Int32Collection myTriangleIndicesCollection =
                    new Int32Collection(new int[] { 0, 1, 2 });

myMeshGeometry3D.TriangleIndices =
                    myTriangleIndicesCollection;
```

Sets the Triangle Indices. Here the first point is (-0.5, 0, -0.5), the second point is (0.5, 0, 0.5), and the third point is (0, 1.5, 0). So the first Indice is from the first point to the second point, from (-0.5, 0, -0.5) to (0.5, 0, 0.5). The second Indice is from the second to the third point, from (0.5, 0, 0.5) to (0, 1.5, 0). The third Indice is from the third to the first point, from (0, 1.5, 0) to (-0.5, 0, -0.5). So this order is set in the TriangleIndices property of MeshGeometry3D class.

The triangle I created has two faces; one is the front, and the other is the back. The rotation direction of the points determines the front face. If the points of a surface are in a counterclockwise direction, then that surface is the front surface, and if the points are in a clockwise direction, then that surface is the back surface. I can assign different materials to the front and back surface of the shape.

Creating the Light Source

The CreateLightSource method creates a light source. The light source is created using the DirectionalLight class. The DirectionalLight class has two properties, one which is the direction of the light and the other is the color of the light. The direction is a Vector3D object specifying which direction the light source should point. Below is the code for the CreateLightSource method.

```
private static DirectionalLight CreateLightSource()
{
    DirectionalLight myDirectionalLight = new DirectionalLight();
    my directional light.Color = Colors.White;
    my directional light.Direction = new Vector3D(-1, -1, -1);
    return myDirectionalLight;
}
```

Creating the Camera Object

The CreateCamera method creates a camera object. The PerspectiveCamera object has three important properties. The first one is the position of the camera in the three-dimensional space. The second one is the LookDirection, which is the direction where the camera focuses. LookDirection is a Vector3D object. The next one is the FieldOfView which is the angle of view. If the FieldOfView is smaller, the shape appears to be big, and if the FieldOfView is larger, the camera becomes a wide-angle camera, and the shape appears small. Below is the full code of the CreateCamera method.

```
private static PerspectiveCamera CreateCamera()
{
    PerspectiveCamera myPCamera = new PerspectiveCamera();
    myPCamera.Position = new Point3D(10, 0.3, 0);
    myPCamera.LookDirection = new Vector3D(-10, 0.3, 0);
    myPCamera.FieldOfView = 20;
    return myPCamera;
}
```

Creating the Material

Material is required to fill the front side and back sides of the shape. Here I use the DiffuseMaterial object as the material. A SolidColorBrush object is created using yellow color, and DiffuseMaterial constructors take the Brush object as a parameter. The material and the BackMaterial shape property value can be set using the DiffuseMaterial object.

```
SolidColorBrush           solidColorBrush          =          new
SolidColorBrush(Colors.Yellow);
DiffuseMaterial           myMaterial               =          new
DiffuseMaterial(solidColorBrush);
myGeometryModel.Material = myMaterial;
myGeometryModel.BackMaterial = myMaterial;
```

Adding the Angle Rotation

In this example, I am rotating the triangle along the Y-axis. The AxisAngleRotation3D object is created with the axis as a point (0, 1, 0). The angle property of the AxisAngleRotation3D object was set as zero. Changing the angle of the AxisAngleRotation3D object makes the coordinates rotate along the y-axis. I can rotate along any axis and also rotate along multiple axes simultaneously. The AxisAngleRotation3D object is set as the value of the Rotation property of the RotateTransform3D object, and the RotateTransform3D object is added to the Transform3DGroup object as a child. Changing the yaxisRotation.Angle value will rotate the coordinates along the y-axis, making the shape or the entire scenery rotate.

```
Transform3DGroup myTransform3DGroup =
                    new Transform3DGroup();

RotateTransform3D myRotateTransform3DY =
                    new RotateTransform3D();

AxisAngleRotation3D yaxisRotation =
                    new AxisAngleRotation3D();

yaxisRotation.Axis = new Vector3D(0, 1, 0);
yaxisRotation.Angle = 0;
myRotateTransform3DY.Rotation = yaxisRotation;
myTransform3DGroup.Children.Add(myRotateTransform3DY);
```

Creating the Animation

The Viewport3D element hosts a 3D model in our application. The Viewport3D is like a canvas on which I can draw 3D objects. The Model3DGroup class groups many 3D models and can apply transformations and animations as a single group.

```
Viewport3D myViewport3D = new Viewport3D();
Model3DGroup myModel3DGroup = new Model3DGroup();
```

GeometryModel3D myGeometryModel =
new GeometryModel3D();

ModelVisual3D myModelVisual3D = new ModelVisual3D();

Here a triangle shape is created with the CreateMeshGeometry method, which I explained earlier. The myMeshGeometry3D object represents the triangle shape.

MeshGeometry3D myMeshGeometry3D =
CreateMeshGeometry();

myGeometryModel.Geometry = myMeshGeometry3D;

After that, a camera object is created using the CreateCamera method and added to the Viewport3D class object as a camera using the below code.

PerspectiveCamera myPCamera = CreateCamera();
myViewport3D.Camera = myPCamera;

Then a DirectionalLight object is created using the CreateLightSource method and added as a child of the Model3DGroup object.

DirectionalLight myDirectionalLight = CreateLightSource();
myModel3DGroup.Children.Add(myDirectionalLight);

In the for loop yaxisRotation.Angle value is incremented by two in every rotation, which rotates the shape by 2 degrees. The Viewport3D and Canvas objects are rendered into Images and saved in each iteration.

```
for (int i = 0; i < 300; i++)
{
    yaxisRotation.Angle = yaxisRotation.Angle + 2;
    ....
}
```

Once the loop is completed, the Images are converted to video by the CreateVideoFromImages method.

```
CreateVideoFromImages("ImageOutput",
                "VideoOutput\\3DTriangle.Mp4");
```

WPF Project Full Code

```
using System;
using System.Diagnostics;
using System.Windows;
using System.Windows.Controls;
using System.Windows.Media;
using System.Windows.Media.Imaging;
using System.Windows.Media.Media3D;


public void CreateVideo()
{
    if (!System.IO.Directory.Exists("ImageOutput"))
        System.IO.Directory.CreateDirectory("ImageOutput");

    if (!System.IO.Directory.Exists("VideoOutput"))
        System.IO.Directory.CreateDirectory("VideoOutput");

    Viewport3D myViewport3D = new Viewport3D();
    Model3DGroup myModel3DGroup = new Model3DGroup();

    GeometryModel3D myGeometryModel =
                        new GeometryModel3D();

    ModelVisual3D myModelVisual3D = new ModelVisual3D();

    PerspectiveCamera myPCamera = CreateCamera();
    myViewport3D.Camera = myPCamera;

    DirectionalLight myDirectionalLight = CreateLightSource();
```

```
myModel3DGroup.Children.Add(myDirectionalLight);

MeshGeometry3D myMeshGeometry3D =
                        CreateMeshGeometry();

myGeometryModel.Geometry = myMeshGeometry3D;

SolidColorBrush solidColorBrush =
                new SolidColorBrush(Colors.Yellow);

DiffuseMaterial myMaterial =
                new DiffuseMaterial(solidColorBrush);

myGeometryModel.Material = myMaterial;
myGeometryModel.BackMaterial = myMaterial;

Transform3DGroup myTransform3DGroup =
    new Transform3DGroup();

RotateTransform3D myRotateTransform3DY =
    new RotateTransform3D();

AxisAngleRotation3D yaxisRotation =
    new AxisAngleRotation3D();

yaxisRotation.Axis = new Vector3D(0, 1, 0);
yaxisRotation.Angle = 0;
myRotateTransform3DY.Rotation = yaxisRotation;
myTransform3DGroup.Children.Add(myRotateTransform3DY);


myGeometryModel.Transform = myTransform3DGroup;
myModel3DGroup.Children.Add(myGeometryModel);
myModelVisual3D.Content = myModel3DGroup;
myViewport3D.Children.Add(myModelVisual3D);
myViewport3D.Arrange(new Rect(0, 0, 1920, 1080));

for (int i = 0; i < 300; i++)
{
    yaxisRotation.Angle = yaxisRotation.Angle + 2;
```

```csharp
            string imageName = ("000000000" + i.ToString());

            imageName =
               imageName.Substring(imageName.Length - 6, 6) +
               ".png";

            RenderTargetBitmap renderTargetBitmap =
               new RenderTargetBitmap(1920, 1080,
               96, 96, PixelFormats.Pbgra32);

            Canvas canvas = new Canvas();
            canvas.Background = Brushes.Lavender;
            canvas.Arrange(new Rect(0, 0, 1920, 1080));
            renderTargetBitmap.Render(canvas);
            renderTargetBitmap.Render(myViewport3D);

            System.IO.FileStream fileStream =
               new System.IO.FileStream("ImageOutput\\" +
               imageName, System.IO.FileMode.Create);

            PngBitmapEncoder pngBitmapEncoder =
               new PngBitmapEncoder();

            pngBitmapEncoder.Frames.Add(
               BitmapFrame.Create(renderTargetBitmap));

            pngBitmapEncoder.Save(fileStream);
            fileStream.Close();
         }
         CreateVideoFromImages("ImageOutput\\",
            "VideoOutput\\3DTriangle.Mp4");
      }


private static MeshGeometry3D CreateMeshGeometry()
{
      MeshGeometry3D myMeshGeometry3D =
      new MeshGeometry3D();
```

```
        Point3DCollection myPositionCollection =
        new Point3DCollection();

        myPositionCollection.Add(
            new Point3D(-0.5, 0, -0.5));

        myPositionCollection.Add(
            new Point3D(0.5, 0, 0.5));

        myPositionCollection.Add(
            new Point3D(0, 1.5, 0));

        myMeshGeometry3D.Positions =
        myPositionCollection;

        Int32Collection myTriangleIndicesCollection =
            new Int32Collection(new int[] { 0, 1, 2 });

        myMeshGeometry3D.TriangleIndices =
            myTriangleIndicesCollection;

        return myMeshGeometry3D;
}


private static DirectionalLight CreateLightSource()
{
    DirectionalLight myDirectionalLight =
        new DirectionalLight();

    myDirectionalLight.Color = Colors.White;

    myDirectionalLight.Direction =
        new Vector3D(-1, -1, -1);

    return myDirectionalLight;
}


private static PerspectiveCamera CreateCamera()
```

```
{
    PerspectiveCamera myPCamera = new PerspectiveCamera();
    myPCamera.Position = new Point3D(10, 0.3, 0);
    myPCamera.LookDirection = new Vector3D(-10, 0.3, 0);
    myPCamera.FieldOfView = 20;
    return myPCamera;
}


public static void CreateVideoFromImages(
        string inputImagesfolder,
        string videoOutputFile)
{
    Process process = new Process();
    process.StartInfo.FileName = "cmd.exe";
    process.StartInfo.Arguments = "/C " + " ffmpeg -i \"" +
        inputImagesfolder +
        "%06d.png\" -y -pix_fmt yuv420p \""
        + videoOutputFile + "\" ";

    process.StartInfo.UseShellExecute = false;
    process.Start();
    process.WaitForExit();

    int exitCode = process.ExitCode;
    if (exitCode == 0)
    {
        Console.WriteLine("Creating Video From" +
            " Images completed successfully!");
    }
    else
    {
        Console.WriteLine($"FFmpeg processing " +
            $"failed with exit code: {exitCode}");
    }
}
```

www.ingramcontent.com/pod-product-compliance
Lightning Source LLC
LaVergne TN
LVHW051335050326
832903LV00031B/3560